DEVOTIONS
+ PRAYERS
for
WARRIOR
WOMEN

DEVOTIONS + PRAYERS
for
WARRIOR WOMEN

INSPIRATION FOR
A COURAGEOUS HEART

Donna K. Maltese

BARBOUR
PUBLISHING

Cover Design: Greg Jackson, Thinkpen Design

Published by Barbour Publishing, Inc., 1810 Barbour Drive, Uhrichsville, Ohio 44683, www.barbourbooks.com

Our mission is to inspire the world with the life-changing message of the Bible.

Member of the
Evangelical Christian
Publishers Association

Printed in China.

INTRODUCTION

*Hallelujah! Praise GOD from heaven, praise him from the
mountaintops; praise him, all you his angels, praise him,
all you his warriors, praise him, sun and moon, praise
him, you morning stars; praise him, high heaven, praise
him, heavenly rain clouds; praise, oh let them praise the
name of GOD—he spoke the word, and there they were!*

PSALM 148:1–5 MSG

You have an inner being, one who craves all the strength, knowledge, wisdom, faith, persistence, and hope God has to offer. And God has a special and specific purpose for your life. But to do what He has called you alone to do, you must have an intimate relationship with Him, seeking Him through His Word and connecting with Him through prayer.

Begin your journey of transforming your inner being into a warrior woman by building up your strength and confidence in God through the two hundred devotions that lie ahead. Each begins with God's Word. Give yourself time to let His message soak into your mind and heart. Absorb the reading that follows, allowing it to give you clarity and insight into your life and Lord. Then let the prayer that follows sink into your spirit as you lift up your being to the Lord who loves you—His warrior woman—and whose blessings are chasing you with every breath you take.

ABOVE ALL

"May the Lord be with you, and may you succeed in
building the house of the Lord your God, as He said about you.
Above all, may the Lord give you insight and understanding. . . .
Be strong and courageous. Don't be afraid or discouraged."

1 Chronicles 22:11–13 hcsb

God had a specific plan for King Solomon: to build His house. The Lord also gave him a godly father, one who told him that what he needed "above all" things was God's insight and understanding, His strength and courage.

God has a specific plan for your life as well. To achieve your purpose, today's scripture reminds you to seek God's presence. To remember that you do not walk alone but with a supernatural and super-strong Spirit who is eager to help and guide you.

Your job, above all other things, is to look to God for His insight and understanding, no matter how big or small the task before you. How do you do that? By reading God's Word and coming to Him in prayer with ears that are ready to listen, a heart that longs to hear His voice, and a spirit that aches for His touch.

The more you seek the Lord, the more you immerse yourself in His words, the more strength and courage you will absorb from His presence.

> LORD, I COME TO YOU FOR YOUR WORDS OF
> WISDOM ABOVE ALL THINGS. GUIDE ME IN
> THE PATH YOU HAVE CREATED BEFORE ME.

ALL YOU NEED

The Master spoke to Paul in a dream: "Keep it up, and don't
let anyone intimidate or silence you. No matter what happens,
I'm with you. . . ." That was all he needed to stick it out.
ACTS 18:9–11 MSG

Whenever the apostle Paul tried to tell the Jews in Corinth about Christ, all they did was argue with him. Exasperated, Paul was ready to give up. He was ready to walk away. To turn aside and venture off, to seek another field in which to plant God's seed.

Then one night the Lord spoke to Paul in a dream. He told him to keep on keeping on. Not to let anyone silence or intimidate him, because, no matter what, God was with him. That's what kept Paul going.

In today's world, many people will try to intimidate you, to tell you to be quiet. In those moments, you may feel your inner warrior woman is faltering. You may begin to wonder if you should remain silent. You may begin to question what God wants you to do. If you are harboring doubts and are ready to walk away from those seeking to intimidate you, open up yourself to God. Pray for direction, for words of reassurance. Do so with the confidence that He will give you all you need to do what you are called to do.

THANK YOU, LORD, FOR WALKING WITH ME.
I PRAY YOU WILL GIVE ME ALL I NEED TO PERSEVERE.

YOUR STORM STILLER

Then they cried out to the Lord in their trouble, and He brought them out of their distress. He stilled the storm to a murmur, and the waves of the sea were hushed. They rejoiced when the waves grew quiet. Then He guided them to the harbor they longed for.

PSALM 107:28–30 HCSB

Got trouble? Is your warrior woman being overrun by waves of worry crashing over her bow? Do you feel as if your inner and outer world is rocking out of control? Does it seem as if your "courage [is] melting away in anguish" (Psalm 107:26 HCSB) and that all your knowledge and skill are useless right now?

If your boat is rocking and you can't find your way through the storm, cry out to God! Garner the expectation that He will bring you out of whatever is distressing you and yours. Know that He has and will use His power to still your storm to a murmur and hush the seas that have been battering you.

Then, when all is still, rejoice and praise Him! And before you know it, you'll find yourself safely guided to the harbor you've been striving for.

LORD, THANK YOU FOR STILLING THE STORMS
WITHIN AND WITHOUT, FOR HUSHING THE
RESTLESS SEAS AROUND ME. FOR GUIDING
ME TO A SAFE HARBOR IN YOU!

A VALIANT WARRIOR

*O God, my heart is fixed (steadfast, in the confidence
of faith); I will sing, yes, I will sing praises, even with my
glory [all the faculties and powers of one created in Your
image]! . . . Through and with God we shall do valiantly,
for He it is Who shall tread down our adversaries.*

PSALM 108:1, 13 AMPC

When you feel as if you can go no further, when what you are going for seems impossible to reach, remember who you are. You are God's woman of faith. Allow yourself to take your confidence and courage in that fact. Then begin to sing praises to the one who has given you life, strength, and a purpose. Remember that you have been created in His image. That by seeking Him before all else, you have tapped into His power. That with Him in your life, nothing is impossible.

Fix your eyes on Jesus. Know that He is your brother. Never forget that you and He share the same parent—God your Father. Acknowledge that His Spirit is residing within you. That He is here to help you every step of the way.

Today and every day, warrior woman, be assured that with God, you will do more than well. You will do valiantly.

I GO FORWARD TODAY WITH CONFIDENCE, LORD,
SINGING PRAISES ALL THE WAY. FOR WITH YOU
IN MY LIFE AND HEART, WITH YOU WALKING
BESIDE ME, I AM A VALIANT WARRIOR!

NEVER SHAKEN

David says in regard to Him, I saw the Lord constantly
before me, for He is at my right hand that I may not be shaken
or overthrown or cast down [from my secure and happy state].

ACTS 2:25 AMPC

Today's verse comes from the eighth verse of Psalm 16, which was written by David, the shepherd boy who became king. The one who, from a human point of view, all too often seemed to have the odds stacked against him. But because David knew and trusted in God, knew He would never abandon him, he kept his eyes and mind on the Lord. By constantly seeing the Lord before him, David's confidence could not help but be affected. For David didn't see himself as a helpless human but as a mighty man of God.

This is the attitude your inner warrior must adopt if she is to have confidence and courage throughout her day. She must trust in God, know He is walking beside her, no matter what others may say or think.

How can you begin adopting such an attitude, remaining unshaken no matter what comes your way? By beginning at the beginning: put your trust in God and take refuge in Him (Psalm 16:1).

I WANT TO BE A WOMAN WHO IS NEVER
SHAKEN, LORD. SO I BEGIN TODAY, PRAYING,
"KEEP AND PROTECT ME, O GOD, FOR IN YOU I
HAVE FOUND REFUGE, AND IN YOU DO I PUT MY
TRUST AND HIDE MYSELF" (PSALM 16:1 AMPC).

REWARD REAPER

*You, who are devoted to being with God and
searching for God, be strong and do not lose
courage because your actions will reap rewards.*

2 CHRONICLES 15:7 VOICE

Every woman needs encouragement, some words to help her get through the day that lies ahead. To that end, the Bible is the greatest resource she can tap in the morning hours, the moments before her feet even hit the floor.

In today's verse, we read the encouragement that a king (specifically, Asa of Judah) received from a prophet (Azariah). In the events preceding this reassurance from one of God's seers, a vast Ethiopian army had come against Judah. As Asa went out to meet it, he prayed, "LORD, there is no one besides You to help the mighty and those without strength. Help us, LORD our God, for we depend on You" (2 Chronicles 14:11 HCSB).

What a prayer! What sweet music to God's ears! Asa had made a choice. To trust in and stay true to God. And because of that choice, he was victorious. He sought the Lord, and so the Lord stuck with him. And his actions reaped rewards.

The same is true of you. If you continually seek God and trust Him, if you stay strong and courageous, your actions will reap rewards.

*I BEGIN MY DAY, LORD, SEEKING YOUR PRESENCE,
GUIDANCE, AND VOICE. I TRUST YOU TO GIVE ME THE
STRENGTH AND COURAGE I NEED TODAY, KNOWING
THAT IN YOU AND FOR YOU I WILL REAP REWARDS!*

STANDING UP

Paul stood up among them and said, "You men should have followed my advice not to sail from Crete and sustain this damage and loss. Now I urge you to take courage, because there will be no loss of any of your lives, but only of the ship."

ACTS 27:21–22 HCSB

Paul was a stand-up guy. Even though the men sailing with him had not followed his advice the first time around—bringing disastrous results—he didn't hold a grudge. He didn't give them the silent treatment. Although an "I told you so" can be read into his monologue, he continues to try to encourage his shipmates.

Paul stands before them, urging his fellow travelers to take courage. Why? Paul explains it like this: "For this night an angel of the God I belong to and serve stood by me, and said, 'Don't be afraid, Paul. You must stand before Caesar. And, look! God has graciously given you all those who are sailing with you' " (Acts 27:23–24 HCSB).

When you are in the middle of restless seas, when you aren't sure of the future, know that God's angel stands beside you. He wants you to know that your Lord is with you with every stroke of the paddle, blessing you with all the courage you need until you reach safe harbor with Him.

THANK YOU, LORD, FOR ALWAYS STANDING BY ME
THROUGH ROUGH WATERS, LEADING ME TO SAFETY.
KNOWING THIS, MAY I HAVE THE COURAGE TO STAND
UP AND ENCOURAGE THOSE TRAVELING WITH ME.

FAITH BIRTHS CONFIDENCE

*"Therefore, take courage, men, because I believe God
that it will be just the way it was told to me. However,
we must run aground on a certain island."*

ACTS 27:25–26 HCSB

Paul and his shipmates were in trouble. Seeing this, a God-sent angel gave Paul a message from God, telling him not to be afraid, for God would graciously save not only Paul, for whom God still had plans, but the men sailing with him too.

It was this message from God in addition to Paul's faith in Him, in His words, that prompted him to share the good news with his shipmates. At the same time, Paul shared the bad news: that their ship would, at some point, run aground on a specific island.

Let's face it. We will experience difficult times in life. But if we have faith—that God will keep His promises. . .that we can trust His words. . .that He sees what's going on in our lives. . .that He is standing beside us. . .that He is sending messengers to encourage us—then we will not only find the strength to endure but a way to encourage others to take heart.

IN YOU, LORD, I BELIEVE. IN YOUR WORDS I
TRUST, KNOWING ALL WILL TURN OUT JUST LIKE
YOU HAVE SAID IT WILL. IN YOU I FIND THE FAITH
TO BUILD THE CONFIDENCE OF OTHERS.

RIPPLE EFFECT OF ENCOURAGEMENT

"I urge you to take some food. For this has to do with your survival,
since none of you will lose a hair from your head." After he said
these things and had taken some bread, he gave thanks to God
in the presence of all of them, and when he broke it, he began to
eat. They all became encouraged and took food themselves.

ACTS 27:34–36 HCSB

You need faith to feed your inner warrior. That's what Paul demonstrates here.

An angel had told Paul to take courage. That he and his shipmates would survive this voyage. That faith gave him the confidence to encourage his fellow travelers not only spiritually but physically. Paul urged them to take food. He assured them that not even one hair on their heads would be lost in the days to come.

Then Paul himself took food, gave thanks to God in their presence, and began to eat. Following his example, the men's despair was transformed into hope.

When you allow your inner woman, your warrior, to take the helm, not only will your outlook improve, but you will give hope and encouragement to all those who witness your faith—your confidence in the Lord who has promised that in the last days not one hair on your head will perish (Luke 21:18).

> LORD, IN YOU I FIND THE COURAGE TO FACE
> ROUGH SEAS AND, AT THE SAME TIME, GIVE
> HOPE AND ENCOURAGEMENT TO OTHERS.

IN HIS IMAGE

"Yahweh your God is among you, a warrior who saves.
He will rejoice over you with gladness. He will bring you
quietness with His love. He will delight in you with shouts of joy."
ZEPHANIAH 3:17 HCSB

You, woman of God, can have all the courage and strength you need to face all your days. All you need to do is remember that Yahweh is with you. He stands right beside you, His Spirit residing within you, His Son holding your hand.

Your God delights in you, rejoices over you. His love encompasses you like a shield, not only protecting you but quieting all the tumult and anxiety that come your way.

God has said that you have been made in His image (Genesis 1:27). This means you too are a warrior among your brothers and sisters. You have the power, infused within you by God, to face difficulties, to fight evil with love, to rise up knowing you are strong enough, good enough, and faithful enough to meet any challenge this world may present.

Today, make it clear in your mind and heart that you, like God, are a warrior.

YAHWEH, YOU ARE SO WONDERFUL TO ME!
THANK YOU FOR INFUSING ME WITH YOUR
STRENGTH. BE WITH ME AS I OVERCOME EVIL
WITH GOOD IN YOUR NAME AND POWER.

SHE ASKED, HE ANSWERED

The LORD answered Isaac's prayer, and Rebekah became
pregnant with twins. But the two children struggled with
each other in her womb. So she went to ask the LORD about it.
"Why is this happening to me?" she asked. And the LORD told her.

GENESIS 25:21–23 NLT

Rebekah was barren for nineteen years. So her husband Isaac prayed, and God answered, allowing Rebekah to become pregnant with not one but two children!

Rebekah's reaction to what she felt within prompted her to seek the Lord for answers. She didn't go to her husband. She didn't go to Abraham. And she didn't go to any other prophet. She went straight to the source. And He answered—in detail (Genesis 25:23).

Know that as a woman of God, you have a resource at your fingertips. He is the one who knows just what's going on in your life, within and without. He is the one who will explain all the nitty-gritty details you want to hear. He is the one who can tell you like it is.

Friends, a sibling, or a parent can be great resources of information. But the one who has the most wisdom, the one who has all the answers, is God, to whom you have 24/7 access.

Wondering why? Go directly to God. He will tell you all you need to know.

YOU, LORD, HAVE ALL THE ANSWERS.
SO HERE'S MY QUESTION. . .

ONE REQUEST

*I have one request, dear friends: Pray for me. Pray strenuously
with and for me—to God the Father, through the power
of our Master Jesus, through the love of the Spirit—
that I will be delivered. . . . Then, God willing,
I'll be on my way. . .with a light and eager heart.*
ROMANS 15:30–32 MSG

How many times have you kept your concerns to yourself because you didn't want to appear vulnerable to others? Or to God? Know this: asking others to pray for you is not a sign of weakness. It's a sign of strength—and faith.

The person asking others to pray for him in today's verses is Paul. And he does so in writing. To the Roman churches, the great man of faith bares his heart and soul, addressing his readers as friends, and simply says, "Pray for me." He asks them to pray on his behalf to God through the power of Jesus and the love of the Spirit.

When you need the help of other believers to seek God's direction, strength, and power for a specific purpose, never hesitate. Bare your soul. Make that one request, adding their prayer strength to your own. You will be amazed at the results.

*HELP ME, LORD, TO BE HUMBLE ENOUGH AND
STRONG ENOUGH TO BARE MY HEART AND SOUL
TO MY FELLOW BELIEVERS AS I ASK FOR THEM
TO ADD THEIR PRAYER POWER TO MINE.*

YOUR LIGHT AND MIGHT

*The Eternal is my light amidst my darkness and my rescue in
times of trouble. So whom shall I fear? He surrounds me with
a fortress of protection. So nothing should cause me alarm.*

PSALM 27:1 VOICE

When you're facing a barrage of trouble, either internal or external,
your greatest place of refuge is in God.

The problems of this world are real. Many can lead us into
danger. Yet if we dwell on our weaknesses, we'll feel like victims
of our circumstances, ones over which we have no control. On
the other hand, if we look to God for insights and as a source of
protection, we'll be able to face things head-on, like the warrior
women He desires us to be.

No matter how bleak things may look, how confusing they may
get, remember that you have God in your midst. You can say to
yourself, as the psalmist does, "God is my light amid all the darkness of this world. He will help me get through whatever trouble
comes my way."

Then, armed with God as your source and force, you can ask
yourself, "So who do I need to fear? No one! Because God is surrounding me with His love and protection, there is nothing in this
world that can truly cause me harm or alarm!"

*YOU, LORD, ARE MY LIGHT AND MIGHT. WITH YOU
SURROUNDING ME, I AM CALM AND CONFIDENT,
NO MATTER WHAT COMES MY WAY!*

THAT QUIET, SECURE PLACE

When besieged, I'm calm as a baby. When all hell
breaks loose, I'm collected and cool. I'm asking GOD for
one thing, only one thing: To live with him in his house
my whole life long. I'll contemplate his beauty; I'll study
at his feet. That's the only quiet, secure place in a noisy
world, the perfect getaway, far from the buzz of traffic.
PSALM 27:3–5 MSG

It's amazing how easy it is to get caught up in the havoc this world raises up, how easy it is to forget that an unseen God is walking this road with us. That's why it's so important to immerse yourself in God, His Word, and His Spirit.

Every day, take time to sit at God's feet. To study and meditate on His Word. To remember that each breath you take is a gift from Him. To live your life knowing that you are merely a pilgrim here, that your eternal home with Him is your true destination. Doing so not only feeds the warrior woman within you but gives you a sense of peace, quiet, and security you can find nowhere else in this world.

I COME BEFORE YOU, LORD, READY TO SIT AT
YOUR FEET, LISTEN TO YOUR VOICE, FEEL YOUR
PRESENCE, BE ENCOMPASSED IN YOUR PEACE.

YOUR ETERNAL COMPANION

My father and mother have deserted me, yet the Eternal
will take me in. O Eternal, show me Your way, shine Your
light brightly on this path, and make it level for me.

PSALM 27:10–11 VOICE

The people who parent you can never be replaced. And losing them, whether it's through death or desertion, can be a real heartbreaker. Not having them here to show you the way, to offer their advice, to give unconditional love can be devastating.

Fortunately for us, we have a parent who will never leave nor forsake us. And that parent is our eternal God. With Him there is no chance of abandonment, in whatever form that may take. With Him we have a constant companion. In Him, we have all the wisdom we could ever crave. By Him we have the infinite solace of never-ending promises.

Yet that's not all! Through God's Spirit, we have all the comfort, strength, and peace we could ever need. And through His Son, we are eternally saved.

So, on those days when you feel weak and all alone, look up. Seek the help and solace of the eternal being who has promised never to leave you. Ask Him for the wisdom you need. Pray that He would light your path and give you strength for the journey.

THANK YOU, LORD, FOR TAKING ME IN,
FOR ALWAYS BEING HERE FOR ME. SHOW ME
THE WAY YOU WOULD HAVE ME GO TODAY.

GOD'S GOODNESS

Yet I am confident I will see the LORD's goodness while I am here in the land of the living. Wait patiently for the LORD. Be brave and courageous. Yes, wait patiently for the LORD.

PSALM 27:13–14 NLT

When your inner warrior woman needs a boost of hope, a ray of sunshine, you might want to speak today's verses to yourself.

When all you can see is the darkness of the day. . . When all you hear seems to be bad news. . . When it looks as if the world is falling apart and there's no relief in sight. . . That's when you want to remind yourself of the other side of the story. That's when you want to make it clear in your mind that no matter how hard life has become, you will see God's goodness here. Today. In this world. On the earth. All you need to do is be assured that God is working in the background. That He does have a plan—a *good* one—and is bringing it to fruition. In this moment, remind your warrior woman to be brave and courageous—and to wait. Just wait. God is on the scene. You *will* see His good!

LORD, HELP ME ETCH TODAY'S VERSES ONTO MY HEART SO THAT MY WARRIOR WOMAN WILL STAY STRONG AND COURAGEOUS AS I WAIT TO WITNESS YOUR GOODNESS HERE IN THE LAND OF THE LIVING.

ISSUES

*She came up behind Him in the throng and touched
His garment, for she kept saying, If I only touch His
garments, I shall be restored to health. And immediately
her flow of blood was dried up at the source.*

MARK 5:27–29 AMPC

A synagogue ruler named Jairus asked Jesus to come and heal his daughter who was at death's door. He agreed to follow Jairus home but found Himself pressed all around by people in the crowd.

Amid that crowd was a woman who'd had an issue of blood for twelve years. She'd spent all her money seeking a cure from doctors, but instead of getting better she had only gotten worse. Yet she'd heard about Jesus—one who heals all. And now here He was, so close. *So close.* She kept saying to herself, *If only I touch His garments, I will be whole once more.*

She reached out, touched Jesus' robe, and was healed *immediately*! Jesus, feeling the power leaving Him, asked who'd touched Him. After some hesitation, the woman meekly came forward, fell at His feet, and told Him her story. Jesus responded by saying, "Daughter, you are well because you dared to believe. Go in peace, and stay well" (Mark 5:34 VOICE).

Got an issue? Seek Jesus with confidence. Humbly fall at His feet. Tell Him your story. Be healed.

> *JESUS, IN YOU I DARE TO BELIEVE.
> IT IS YOU ALONE I SEEK. TO YOU I COME.*

REPLACE FEAR WITH FAITH

Do not be seized with alarm and struck
with fear; only keep on believing.
MARK 5:36 AMPC

Before Jesus had been touched by the woman with the issue of blood, He'd been approached by Jairus, a synagogue leader. He asked Jesus to heal his twelve-year-old daughter who lay at death's door. Jesus had agreed and began to follow Jairus home.

But then this woman approached Jesus and surreptitiously touched Him. When He stopped to ask who'd touched Him, the woman came forward and Jesus paused to listen to her story.

Jairus must have been anxiously and impatiently waiting for Jesus to continue on His way. Then, the worst happened. While Jesus was still speaking to the now-healed woman, Jairus' servants came to tell the synagogue leader that his daughter was dead. No need to bother the healer now.

Jesus, overhearing this conversation, told Jairus to replace his fear with faith: "Don't be afraid; just believe" (Mark 5:36 VOICE). In the end, Jesus raised up Jairus' daughter, taking her by the hand and saying, "Little girl, it's time to wake up" (Mark 5:41 VOICE). In that instant, she opened her eyes and rose from her bed.

No matter how many interruptions break into your time with Jesus, no matter how many times your hope becomes fractured because things aren't happening quickly enough, stay courageous. Simply keep on believing.

LORD, HELP ME NOT TO BE FROZEN
BY FEAR BUT TO KEEP ON BELIEVING,
KNOWING YOUR HELP IS ON ITS WAY.

DETERMINATION

Ruth replied, "Don't ask me to leave you and turn back.
Wherever you go, I will go; wherever you live, I will live.
Your people will be my people, and your God will be my
God. . . . May the LORD punish me severely if I allow anything
but death to separate us!" When Naomi saw that Ruth
was determined to go with her, she said nothing more.
RUTH 1:16–18 NLT

The Moabitess' life had entered crisis mode. Ruth's father-in-law, brother-in-law, and husband had died, leaving a household of women bereft of a male protector and provider in a very male-dominated society. Now her mother-in-law, Naomi, was insisting on leaving Moab and walking back to her hometown of Bethlehem.

Naomi had already convinced her daughter-in-law Orpah to go back to her father's house. But Ruth had other ideas. She, in so many words, told Naomi that she'd be sticking to her like glue—that only death would ever separate them. And Naomi finally acquiesced.

That's the kind of determination a warrior woman must have if she's to be successful, if she is to live her life God's way and allow nothing but His will, Word, and way to deter her from whatever path she takes. For it is by this route alone that she will prosper—in her eyes and God's!

LORD, I PRAY YOU WOULD FILL ME WITH ALL
THE DETERMINATION I NEED TO STICK TO THE
PURPOSE YOU HAVE PLACED BEFORE ME.

YOUR RESCUING KNIGHT

*GOD is bedrock under my feet, the castle in which I live,
my rescuing knight. My God—the high crag where I run for
dear life, hiding behind the boulders, safe in the granite hideout;
my mountaintop refuge, he saves me from ruthless men. I sing
to GOD the Praise-Lofty, and find myself safe and saved.*

2 SAMUEL 22:1–4 MSG

All warriors need help every now and then, from both their fellow warriors and almighty God. David found this out just before he wrote this "song of praise to the Eternal because He delivered him from all of his enemies and especially from Saul" (2 Samuel 22:1 VOICE).

David became exhausted when fighting Philistine giants. Then "Ishbi-Benob, a warrior descended from Rapha, with a spear weighing nearly eight pounds and outfitted in brand-new armor, announced that he'd kill David. But Abishai son of Zeruiah came to the rescue, struck the Philistine, and killed him" (2 Samuel 21:16–17 MSG).

Even though David had been saved by a fellow human, he praised God, the source of all things, the rock beneath his feet, his rescuing knight.

When you're tired, run to God. Hide in Him when powers come against you. Know that in God alone, you, His warrior woman, are safe.

*THANK YOU, LORD, FOR BEING MY KNIGHT IN
SHINING ARMOR. UPON YOU, MY ROCK, I STAND.
IN YOU I HIDE, SAFE, SAVED, AND LOVED.*

AN AUDIENCE OF ONE

A hostile world! I called to GOD, to my God I cried out.
From his palace he heard me call; my cry brought me
right into his presence—a private audience!
2 SAMUEL 22:7 MSG

This world can be a very harsh and difficult place, especially for pilgrims like you who know this is not your true home. Yet you never need to worry about the safety of your soul, the sanctity of your spirit. For there is a place you can run to when you need help, healing, and hope.

Call out to God when things get tough. Remember that even warrior women need help sometimes. Know that when you do call God's name, you are immediately swept into His presence, covered by His protective arms, hidden until you can recover your sanity and strength.

There is no better place to be.

Now, in this moment, call out to God. Imagine Him hearing you from His heavenly palace. Then feel yourself transported into His presence. It is now thee and He, alone. Rest there. Then open your ears and listen to His words of comfort and direction. Allow Him to refresh and restore your inner warrior.

> TO YOU I CALL, LORD. HEAR MY CRY.
> WHISK ME INTO YOUR PRESENCE.

CAUGHT IN GOD'S LOVE

But me he caught—reached all the way from sky to sea;
he pulled me out of that ocean of hate, that enemy chaos,
the void in which I was drowning. They hit me when I
was down, but GOD stuck by me. He stood me up on a
wide-open field; I stood there saved—surprised to be loved!

2 SAMUEL 22:17–20 MSG

When you are in trouble, never fear. God will reach down from heaven, pull you out of the turbulent waters, catch you up in His hand, and whisk you away from the chaos, the void in which you feel you are drowning.

God will then gently set you down in an open field where you can catch your breath. As you bask in His love and light, you'll find your nerves soothed, your head clear, your spirit refreshed, your warrior woman ready to do what she is called to do once more.

Then, in a flash of insight, you will realize that you are being cushioned in God's love. As surprising as that may seem, that love is always there for you. All you need to do is lift yourself up to the one who created you, the one who delights in you, the one who continually saves you.

THANK YOU, LORD, FOR ALWAYS BEING THERE,
FOR LOVING ME NO MATTER WHAT.

LIGHTS ON!

Suddenly, GOD, your light floods my path, GOD drives
out the darkness. I smash the bands of marauders,
I vault the high fences. What a God! His road stretches
straight and smooth. Every GOD-direction is road-tested.
Everyone who runs toward him makes it.

2 SAMUEL 22:29–31 MSG

Darkness can sometimes seem to overtake the light. Those are the times when we have been rejected, abandoned, disrespected, used, and abused. When despair begins to overwhelm you and your spirit starts to sink, when the inner warrior woman seems to be cowering in the corner, remember that you are God's daughter—and all you need to do is bring Him to mind and heart.

Before you know it, His light will be flooding your pathway. There's no more stumbling around in the dark. Now you can do all that He is calling you to do—and more! Why? Because you are on His path. You have embarked upon His way. And He has gone before you, leaving you road signs to follow.

The way before you now is not only illuminated but straight and smooth. No more tripping up! You are God's. And because you are, you will not just succeed but prosper!

YOU, LORD, HAVE BROUGHT ME OUT OF THE SHADOWS.
NOW I SEE THE PATH YOU HAVE LAID OUT BEFORE ME.
BECAUSE YOU ARE IN MY LIFE, I AND THE WARRIOR
WOMAN WITHIN ME ARE ABLE TO DO ANYTHING!

WELL-ARMED

Is there any god like GOD? Are we not at bedrock? Is not
this the God who armed me well, then aimed me in the right
direction? Now I run like a deer; I'm king of the mountain.
He shows me how to fight; I can bend a bronze bow! You
protect me with salvation-armor; you touch me and I
feel ten feet tall. You cleared the ground under me so my
footing was firm. . . . You armed me well for this fight.
2 SAMUEL 22:32–37, 40 MSG

Have you ever felt ill equipped to do what God is calling you to do? Have you ever turned to Him and said, "Really, Lord? Me? You want *me* to walk this road?"

When your inner warrior woman needs encouragement and strength, remember who your Lord is. He's the one who can part the waters and bring them back together again. He's the one who can heal any issue you have, turn water into wine, make the earth tremble and hills roll. Your God is the one who created everything you see—and everything you don't see!

And He has called you (yes, you!) for a specific purpose. Thus, you can be sure you have all you need to do what others may think is impossible. But with God it is totally doable.

THANK YOU, LORD, FOR ARMING ME WELL FOR THE ROAD BEFORE ME. THERE IS NO GOD LIKE YOU!

WARRIOR WOMAN SAVES THE ROYAL SEED

When Ahaziah's mother Athaliah saw that her son was dead,
she took over. She began by massacring the entire royal family.
Jehosheba, daughter of King Jehoram, took Ahaziah's son Joash,
and kidnapped him from among the king's sons slated for slaughter.
2 CHRONICLES 22:10–11 MSG

Here we are presented with two women. The first, Athaliah, was the personification of evil. Once her son, King Ahaziah, was dead, she went on a murderous rampage, killing every one of the royal seed of Judah—except one. The second woman, Jehosheba, was the half sister of the king and wife of Jehoiada the priest. When she realized that Athaliah was going to kill the Judean royals, thus wiping out the line from which God had promised an eternal king, her inner warrior woman kicked into gear.

With extreme calm and courage, Jehosheba kidnapped Joash, King Ahaziah's infant son, and his nurse from among the sons "slated for slaughter." She then hid the two for six years in the temple of God. Because of her courage, the royal seed and line of Judah lived on.

Whenever you need encouragement, read Jehosheba's story, remembering that God supplies His warrior women with all the mettle they need to do mighty deeds!

YOU, LORD, ARE THE GREAT ENABLER! THANK YOU
FOR THIS AMAZING EXAMPLE OF A WARRIOR SISTER!

AT YOUR SIDE

"Take charge! Take heart! Don't be anxious or
get discouraged. GOD, my God, is with you in this;
he won't walk off and leave you in the lurch.
He's at your side until every last detail is completed."

1 CHRONICLES 28:20 MSG

No matter where you go, God is with you. He has promised never to leave you nor forsake you (Deuteronomy 31:6–8). And, unlike humans, God keeps His word. So God never abandoning you is not just a promise but a fact.

Etch the words of 1 Chronicles 28:20 on your mind and heart. They will be a constant reminder to you that you need not fear anything. Just simply roll up your sleeves and do the work. When things get jammed up or people let you down, remember that God is still on your side, rooting for you, cheering you on, Warrior Woman, knowing that what you set your mind and heart to can be accomplished.

God will never walk off the job, leaving you in the lurch. He'll be with you, helping you, encouraging you until the assignment He has placed in your hands is complete.

So go, girl! You've got this!

KNOWING, LORD, THAT YOU WILL NEVER LEAVE
ME BUT WILL STICK BY MY SIDE UNTIL MY
WORK IS DONE IS ALL THE INCENTIVE I AND MY
INNER WARRIOR WOMAN NEED TO DO WHAT
YOU HAVE CALLED US TO DO! LET'S GO!

SUCH A TIME

"Don't be fooled. Just because you are living inside the king's palace doesn't mean that you out of all of the Jews will escape the carnage. You must go before your king. If you stay silent during this time, deliverance for the Jews will come from somewhere, but you, my child, and all of your father's family will die. And who knows? Perhaps you have been made queen for such a time as this."

<small>ESTHER 4:13–14 VOICE</small>

Esther was queen of Persia, living in the palace in Susa, keeping her Jewish heritage a secret. Her cousin Mordecai, who had raised, fed, and sheltered her, sat at the king's gate. He'd been told that a wicked man named Haman had gotten King Ahasuerus to sign a decree to kill all the Jews in the kingdom of Persia.

So Mordecai sent word to Esther to speak to the king about the death sentence hanging over their people. But Esther hesitated. For if a person went before the king without having been summoned, it could mean death.

You too are here, living in such a time as this, when God needs you to do what He has already prepared for you to do. So draw on the courage He provides to do what needs to be done.

I ASK YOU, LORD, TO PROVIDE THE COURAGE I NEED TO DO WHAT YOU HAVE CALLED ME TO DO AT SUCH A TIME AS THIS.

PREP WORK

"In preparation for my audience with the king, do this:
gather together all the Jews in Susa, and fast and pray
for me. Intercede for me. For three days and nights,
abstain from all food and drink. My maids and I will
join you in this time. And after the three days, I will go
in to the king and plead my people's case, even though
it means breaking the law. And if I die, then I die!"
ESTHER 4:16 VOICE

Esther is intelligent. She knows what and who she is up against. She knows the stakes. Now it is time to draw on the power that comes from prayer—the ones that you pray and the ones that others pray for both you and the situation you face.

Esther makes clear the danger she's in by going to the king unsummoned. Yet she also knows that God has a plan for her life. That although deliverance could come from some other quarter, this is Esther's part to play, the part God has prepared her for.

When you need to find your calm and courage to nurture that warrior woman within, tap into the power of prayer.

LORD, I AM YOUR SERVANT. WHERE YOU LEAD,
I WILL FOLLOW. I COME TO YOU IN PRAYER,
READYING MYSELF TO DO WHAT YOU HAVE CALLED
ME TO DO. BATHE MY MISSION IN YOUR GRACE.

CONSEQUENCES
OF COURAGE

As soon as the king saw Queen Esther standing
in the courtyard, she won his approval. The king
extended the gold scepter in his hand toward Esther,
and she approached and touched the tip of the scepter.
"What is it, Queen Esther?" the king asked her. "Whatever
you want, even to half the kingdom, will be given to you."
ESTHER 5:2–3 HCSB

God had called Esther to risk her life for her people. She had bathed this mission in prayer. And with God's courage and calm, Esther did what she had to do at such a time as this.

In response to Esther's obedience to God's calling, her husband, the king, not only welcomed her to come into his presence, but he offered her whatever she wanted—even up to half his kingdom! And at the end of her story, Esther not only makes her Jewish heritage public knowledge but also saves her people! *And* she is rewarded with property while her cousin Mordecai is promoted to the position of prime minister of Persia!

When you step out in faith, determined to do what God has called you to do, regardless of the consequences, prepare to be amazed at the results, rewards, and blessings that follow.

THANK YOU, LORD, GIVING ME THE COURAGE
TO STEP OUT IN FAITH, AND FOR THE
REWARDS AND BLESSINGS THAT FOLLOW.

STRENGTH AND COURAGE COMMANDED

*Have not I commanded you? Be strong, vigorous,
and very courageous. Be not afraid, neither be dismayed.*
JOSHUA 1:9 AMPC

Imagine this scenario. . .

Your mentor is no more. Now it's time for you to take up the mantle of leadership—of one (yourself) or many. So God comes to you to boost the strength and courage of your inner warrior woman.

From the beginning of God's speech to the end, He tells you that you will never walk alone: "I will be with you. . . . I will not fail you or abandon you. . . . The LORD your God is with you wherever you go" (Joshua 1:5, 9 NLT).

How would your life change if you lived it knowing that God is with you *all the time*? That through good days—joyful reunions, peaceful moments, sudden breakthroughs, times of health—God is by your side; and through bad days—uncomfortable encounters, stressful situations, weakness, illness, conflicts, and confrontations—He is still sticking to you like glue?

Part of being a warrior woman is believing, knowing for a fact, that God will not desert you. That amid joy and sorrow, you can continue to praise the one who will never abandon you. Having that mindset is key to keeping you strong and courageous.

*KNOWING THAT YOU, LORD, ARE ALWAYS BY MY
SIDE GIVES ME THE STRENGTH AND COURAGE TO
ENDURE ANYTHING AND EVERYTHING. THANK YOU!*

STRENGTH AND COURAGE TO LEAD

"Be strong and courageous, for you are the one
who will lead these people to possess all the land
I swore to their ancestors I would give them."
JOSHUA 1:6 NLT

You may not consider yourself a leader—but you are, even if you are leading only one person: you. God has filled His Word with an abundant number of promises. But you must be strong enough and brave enough to realize them.

God has paved out a path for you. And in that path will be some obstacles to get over, under, around, or through. Some challenges will also be sprinkled in for good measure. All of these devices are to help strengthen you, to mold you into the warrior woman God created you to be.

Just as God told Joshua he was to lead God's people into Israel (the promised land), so you too must take a step of faith into God's land of promises. You may have to battle old and bad habits. You may have to wend your way through a flood of conflict. You may even have to make a lot of noise to take down some walls. But with God by your side, you can and will find the strength and courage to possess your promised land step-by-step.

LEAD ME, LORD, SO THAT I MAY FOLLOW,
AND PERHAPS EVEN LEAD OTHERS, AND TAKE
HOLD OF YOUR LAND OF PROMISES.

STRENGTH AND COURAGE TO LIVE BY LOVE

Always be strong and courageous, and always live by all of the law I gave to my servant Moses, never turning from it—even ever so slightly—so that you may succeed wherever you go.
JOSHUA 1:7 VOICE

For the second time in His instructions to Joshua, God tells Joshua to be strong and courageous. But here He adds something more. Joshua is *always*—not just some days but every moment of every day—to live by the law God gave to Moses.

How do you follow Moses' law? By following the two commands Jesus gave us. For "the entire law and all the demands of the prophets are based on these two commandments" (Matthew 22:40 NLT). And what are these commandments? " 'You must love the LORD your God with all your heart, all your soul, and all your mind.' This is the first and greatest commandment. A second is equally important: 'Love your neighbor as yourself' " (Matthew 22:37–39 NLT).

Warrior women are built on love. They are strengthened and encouraged by love. It is love that shields them (Psalm 5:12 NLT), love that holds them (Psalm 27:10; Isaiah 41:13, 46:4), love that spurs them into overcoming evil with good (Romans 12:21). In love they are created, live, breathe, and pass on to an eternal life.

Walk in the path of love, and you will meet with success wherever God would have you go.

*HELP ME, LORD, TO LIVE IN LOVE
WITH STRENGTH AND COURAGE.*

STRENGTH AND COURAGE TO MAKE THE WORD YOUR WAY

Let the words from the book of the law be always on your lips.
Meditate on them day and night so that you may be careful to
live by all that is written in it. If you do, as you make your way
through this world, you will prosper and always find success.

JOSHUA 1:8 VOICE

God gives Joshua this last bit of advice in Joshua 1: sink yourself—mind, body, soul, and spirit—into His Word.

Here God is reminding all His warriors that just a quick glance or reading of a devotion won't cut it. To have success, to stay strong and courageous, to live the life God has created you to live and do the deeds He has already prepared you to do, you must memorize the Word. Study it. Write it on the whiteboard of your mind—with permanent marker.

Think about God's Word day and night. In the morning, after reading the Bible, write the verses that speak to your heart. Underline the words that have touched you the most. Then call them to mind as you go throughout your day. This will help you to live by God's Word. This will bring you spiritual prosperity and success as you make your way through this world.

HELP ME, LORD, TO WRITE YOUR WORD UPON MY
HEART, MIND, SPIRIT, AND SOUL, SO THAT I WILL
MEET WITH SUCCESS AS I WALK MY WAY IN YOU!

RIZPAH, WARRIOR WOMAN: PART 1

Abner took advantage of the continuing war between the house of Saul and the house of David to gain power for himself. Saul had had a concubine, Rizpah, the daughter of Aiah. One day Ish-Bosheth confronted Abner: "What business do you have sleeping with my father's concubine?"

2 SAMUEL 3:7 MSG

Rizpah's trials and tragedies had been spawned, for the most part, through the sins of King Saul. She had been his concubine, fathering two of his sons. Heaven only knows the sorrow she must have felt when Saul killed himself and the Philistines cut off his head. Soon after, she was appropriated by Abner, the cousin of Saul and the commander of his army. Abner may have made this move in his hunger for power, for in that place and time, the wives and concubines of a king became the property of the one who inherited the crown.

Ish-Bosheth's (Saul's son and his successor) and Abner's quarrel over Rizpah led to a rift that was never healed. Later Abner was slain by Joab.

Many women find themselves caught up in the strife and war within and between peoples, and are soon bereft of protection, provision, and family. Rizpah was such a person. Yet perhaps these events prepared her with the strength and courage she would need in the days ahead.

LORD, WHEN THINGS HAPPEN OUT OF MY CONTROL, MAY THEY SERVE NOT TO UNNERVE ME BUT TO MAKE ME STRONGER AND BOLDER FOR YOU.

RIZPAH, WARRIOR WOMAN: PART 2

"As for the man who annihilated us and plotted to destroy
us so we would not exist within the whole territory
of Israel, let seven of his male descendants be
handed over to us so we may hang them."
2 SAMUEL 21:5–6 HCSB

During David's kingship, there was a three-year famine. He suspected it had something to do with the late King Saul violating an oath that Joshua had made to the Gibeonites, swearing not to kill them.

To appease the Gibeonites, David accepted their terms, promising to hand over seven of Saul's descendants, two of whom were the sons of the late king and Rizpah. All seven were hanged on the mountain at the beginning of a barley harvest.

Rizpah, having lost her king, was now bereft of her sons as well. So she did what was in her power to do. She spread sackcloth on the rock and kept the birds away from the bodies by day and the wild animals by night. She did this for five months, at the end of which time David heard about her vigil and had the remains of the hanged men's bodies buried with King Saul's.

Like Rizpah, do what right things you can when you can with the strength and courage God gives you.

MAY THE WARRIOR WOMAN WITHIN ME, LORD,
HAVE THE STRENGTH AND COURAGE TO DO THE
RIGHT THING AND OVERCOME THE WRONG.

POWER UP!

God is strong, and he wants you strong. So take everything
the Master has set out for you, well-made weapons of the
best materials. And put them to use so you will be able
to stand up to everything the Devil throws your way.
EPHESIANS 6:10–11 MSG

You can be a warrior woman for God no matter how young or old you are. Whether you are in or out of shape, God can use you on His team to stand up against all the devil's schemes—and he has a million of them. That's why the Word tells you to "be strong in the Lord [be empowered through your union with Him]; draw your strength from Him [that strength which His boundless might provides]" (Ephesians 6:10 AMPC).

God already has a supply of all the strength you'll ever need. And that supply is never ending. To become a warrior woman, one who is strong enough to overcome evil, you must put on every piece of armor God provides. For this "battle is not against flesh and blood, but against the rulers, against the authorities, against the world powers of this darkness, against the spiritual forces of evil in the heavens" (Ephesians 6:12 HCSB).

It's time to draw all the strength from God you can. Ready? Begin!

I'M COMING UP CLOSE TO YOU, LORD. MAY I BE SO
UNITED TO YOU IN SPIRIT, MIND, HEART, AND SOUL
THAT I DON'T KNOW WHERE YOU END AND I BEGIN!

WEAPONS ISSUED

*Take all the help you can get, every weapon
God has issued, so that when it's all over but
the shouting you'll still be on your feet.*
EPHESIANS 6:13 MSG

God has provided all the armor you, as a warrior woman, need to stand your ground. It's up to you to daily adorn yourself with these things: "truth banded around your waist, righteousness as your chest plate, and feet protected in preparation to proclaim the good news of peace. Don't forget to raise the shield of faith above all else, so you will be able to extinguish flaming spears hurled at you from the wicked one. Take also the helmet of salvation and the sword of the Spirit, which is the word of God" (Ephesians 6:14–17 VOICE).

How do you become adorned in truth, righteousness, peace, faith, and salvation? You "learn how to apply them [because] you'll need them throughout your life. God's Word is an indispensable weapon" (Ephesians 6:14–17 MSG).

Today, consider what armor you're wearing. Then think about what qualities you may need to know more about so that you can learn how to apply them in your everyday life.

Remember, God can equip you with what you need. But you're the one who must use what He supplies.

THANK YOU, LORD, FOR ALL THAT YOU PROVIDE. HELP ME, YOUR WARRIOR WOMAN, TO DIG DEEP INTO YOUR WORD SO I CAN DRESS MYSELF UP IN YOUR ARMOR.

STRENGTH FROM FAITH

*At that time, Deborah the prophetess, wife of Lappidoth,
served as judge over Israel. She used to sit beneath the
palm tree of Deborah, situated in the hill country of
Ephraim between Ramah and Bethel, and the people
would go up to her there to settle disputes.*

JUDGES 4:4–5 VOICE

Whenever you feel like you have too much going on in your life to be a warrior woman, consider Deborah. In the days before there were kings of Israel, Deborah was appointed as a judge by the common consent of the people. She was also a prophetess, a wife, and most likely a mother!

Deborah, a very strong and courageous woman, was a judge when King Jabin of Canaan was terrorizing God's people. He had a general named Sisera who had nine hundred iron chariots, which he used to oppress the Israelites for twenty years.

So Deborah sent for a military leader named Barak and told him, "The Eternal God of Israel commands you: 'Go and get into position near Mount Tabor. Take 10,000 soldiers from the tribes of Naphtali and Zebulun. I will draw out Sisera, Jabin's general, to meet you at the wadi Kishon with his chariots and his army, and I will deliver him to you' " (Judges 4:6–7 VOICE). But Barak refused to go without her.

The faith of a warrior woman named Deborah became the strength Israel needed.

**LORD, MAY MY FAITH BECOME THE STRENGTH
OTHERS NEED IN GOOD TIMES AND BAD.**

TRUSTING GOD'S WORD

I will certainly go with you, but you should know
from the beginning that this battle will not lead to
your personal glory. The Eternal has decreed that
the mighty Sisera will be defeated by a woman.

JUDGES 4:9 VOICE

God had commanded a military man named Barak to face General Sisera of Canaan in battle. But Barak would only go if Deborah accompanied him. So she did. But she gave him a warning: the credit for defeating the mighty Sisera would not go to Barak but to a woman.

We are never told why Barak wouldn't go without Deborah. Some Bible scholars say it was his lack of faith. Others say Barak wanted Deborah with him so that he could ask her advice or to inspire his men with her courage. Hebrews 11:32 praises Barak's strength of faith for leading the army with Deborah by his side. But the fact that he didn't have enough trust in God's word to do the job on his own shows the weakness of that faith.

To be a strong and courageous warrior woman, we, like Deborah, must take God at His word. We must put all our faith into the promises He sprinkles throughout the scriptures, then do whatever He calls us to do and leave the rest to Him.

LORD, HELP ME GROW MY TRUST IN YOUR
WORD SO THAT I MIGHT FOLLOW WHERE YOU
LEAD AND LEAVE THE REST UP TO YOU.

PREVAILING FAITH

*Sisera had fled to the tent of Jael, the wife of Heber the Kenite,
and he must have thought himself safe at last, since there was
peace between Jabin, the king of Hazor, and Heber the Kenite.*
JUDGES 4:17 VOICE

All of Sisera's army and chariots were thrown into a panic by the
Eternal. All died by the sword—all except for Sisera. He managed
to escape, running for his life and right into the tent of Heber,
thinking himself "safe at last."

Jael, Heber's wife, invited Sisera inside her dwelling, telling him
there was nothing to fear. She gave him some milk to drink and
covered him with a rug to hide him from whoever might come to
the tent looking for him. After telling Jael to guard the door and
to keep his presence a secret from all who came calling, Sisera fell
into a deep sleep. It was then that Jael crept over to him and
hammered a tent peg into his temple and down into the ground,
killing him.

Later, when Barak came searching for the great general Sisera,
Jael invited him into her tent so that he could see what remained
of this mortal man.

Through Deborah and Jael, God's purpose and their faith
prevailed, bringing His vision into reality. One a judge, the other
a wife, became the warrior women God created them to be. What
about you?

**GOD, HELP ME BECOME A WARRIOR WOMAN
SO THAT YOUR PURPOSE WILL PREVAIL!**

THE SONG OF DEBORAH

LORD, may all your enemies perish as Sisera did.
But may those who love Him be like the
rising of the sun in its strength.
JUDGES 5:31 HCSB

When you fear moving forward, to the place where God would have you go, remember that God has not only promised you victory, but "in fact, He has already gone out ahead of you" (Judges 4:14 VOICE). This is what Deborah believed deeply. Her faith, combined with God's plan and provision, enabled her to be a wife, prophetess, judge, and warrior.

We know less about Jael, since she was described simply as the wife of Heber. But we do know that Deborah, who "arose to be a mother to Israel" (Judges 5:7 VOICE) and went when God called, sang of Jael, "Most blessed of women is she, favored above all women who dwell in tents! . . . At her feet [Sisera] fell, he dropped, and where he dropped, there he lay dead" (Judges 5:24, 27 VOICE).

Hopefully, we'll never have occasion to kill God's enemy, for we are to overcome evil with good (Romans 12:21). But there will be occasions when we will need to overcome our doubts, dig deep into our faith, and be the warrior women God has called us to be—as mothers, wives, students, teachers, office workers, laborers, writers, or whatever God ordains—and as such, become "like the rising of the sun in its strength."

LORD, HELP ME DIG DEEP INTO MY FAITH AND
BECOME YOUR COURAGEOUS WARRIOR WOMAN.

KEEPING THE WAY

The king of Egypt had a talk with the two Hebrew midwives;
one was named Shiphrah and the other Puah. He said,
"When you deliver the Hebrew women, look at the sex
of the baby. If it's a boy, kill him; if it's a girl, let her
live." But the midwives had far too much respect for
God and didn't do what the king of Egypt ordered.
EXODUS 1:15–17 MSG

The current pharaoh knew nothing of the history of the now-dead Joseph and how he, an Israelite, saved Egypt by his wisdom. All Pharaoh could see was that the enslaved Israelite population kept increasing. No matter how horribly the overseers treated them, they continued to thrive.

So, motivated by fear, Pharaoh ordered two Hebrew midwives to kill newborn boys but allow the girls to live. But Shiphrah and Puah had more respect for God than fear of Pharaoh, so they let the baby boys live.

Like these two midwives, a warrior woman is motivated by faith, not fear. She remembers that God's rule, His way, His path is the one she is to follow, above any human ruler, no matter how high up the chain of command.

Before making a decision, consider your motivation and whose rule you're following. If all is aligned with God, you know the path is clear and whatever you need from your inner warrior woman will help you keep to His way.

MAY MY FAITH IN YOU, LORD, CONQUER ANY FEAR.

FAITH AFLOAT

About this time, a man and woman from the tribe of
Levi got married. The woman became pregnant and
gave birth to a son. She saw that he was a special
baby and kept him hidden for three months.

EXODUS 2:1–2 NLT

Jochebed had given birth to a baby boy who she knew in her mother's heart was special. Because of Pharaoh's edict to kill Hebrew boys at birth, she kept her son hidden for three months. When that no longer became feasible, she waterproofed a basket, placed her child inside of it, and "laid it among the reeds along the bank of the Nile River" (Exodus 2:3 NLT).

Imagine how careful Jochebed must have been to keep this boy's birth a secret. And then to have to set him afloat after nursing him, loving him, holding him for three entire months. Yet what faith Jochebed had to put him afloat in the Nile, literally leaving him in God's hands.

Both Jochebed and her husband, Amram, were from the priestly tribe of Levi. Their lives were built on their faith in God, giving Jochebed the strength and courage to put her helpless child in God's hands, praying His will be done.

When you have a hard choice to make, do what you can with what you have. Then leave the results in God's hands.

HELP MY INNER WARRIOR WOMAN, LORD,
TO TRUST YOU WITH ALL THINGS, GREAT AND
SMALL, LEAVING THEM IN YOUR HANDS.

FAITHFULNESS REWARDED

*Then she put the child in it and laid it among the rushes by
the brink of the river [Nile]. And his sister [Miriam] stood
some distance away to learn what would be done to him.*

EXODUS 2:3–4 AMPC

In faith Jochebed laid her infant son in a basket and set him afloat
in the Nile. And in faith the sister stood, watching from a distance,
to see what happened to him.

When Pharaoh's daughter came down to the water to bathe
in the Nile, she saw the basket and learned what was inside. "She
took pity on him and said, This is one of the Hebrews' children!"
(Exodus 2:6 AMPC).

Miriam took this as her signal to ask if one of the Hebrew women
could nurse him for the princess. Pharaoh's daughter agreed. Soon
Miriam was back with her mother Jochebed, who consented to the
princess' offer to take wages for nursing the baby—her own sweet
child!—until he was weaned.

Jochebed and Miriam didn't let fear rule their lives but depended
on the providence of God to make a way where they could see
none. They lived with the quiet expectation that God would do
something worthy of Himself. Because of that expectation, they
were rewarded.

LORD, HELP ME NOT TO LIVE IN FEAR BUT IN QUIET
EXPECTATION OF YOU MOVING IN A MIRACULOUS WAY.

THROUGH THE TEARS

Then they all went to their homes. Mary, however, stood
outside the tomb sobbing, crying, and kneeling at its entrance.
As she cried, two heavenly messengers appeared before
her sitting where Jesus' head and feet had been laid.

JOHN 20:10–12 VOICE

Mary Magdalene had gone to the tomb that held Jesus' dead body. But when she got there, what remained of Him had gone! She ran and told disciples John and Peter that she couldn't find her beloved Jesus. They ran back with her, saw the empty tomb, and returned home confused.

Yet Mary lingered. She stood outside the tomb crying. While doing so, two angels appeared before her, asking her why she was sobbing. She said, "They have taken away my Lord, and I cannot find Him" (John 20:13 VOICE).

Jesus, resurrected, appeared before her, but she didn't recognize Him. He too asked her why she was crying. Thinking He was the gardener, she asked if He'd carried Jesus away. Her desire was to retrieve Him.

Then Jesus called her name: "Mary." And suddenly, filled with joy, Mary recognized and began to worship her beloved.

Allow your inner warrior woman to seek Jesus, even through your tears. When you do, you will find Him.

JESUS, I WILL SEEK YOU, EVEN WHEN CRYING,
KNOWING THAT WHEN I TURN AND LOOK FOR
YOU, YOU WILL BE THERE, CALLING MY NAME.

JESUS' COMPASSION

As soon as the Lord saw her,
He felt compassion for her.
LUKE 7:13 VOICE

Jesus told us that we would have many troubles and sorrows but that we need not fear because He has overcome the world (John 16:33). Jesus can give us the peace we need to carry on, to find the calm we crave. Why? Because He sees us. He sees all we're going through, and His heart swells with compassion for us.

Consider the troubles and sorrows you have endured and may right now be facing. Know that Jesus looks upon you with love and adoration. In no way does He want you to suffer. He may produce a miracle in your life, as He did with the widow whose son had died, raising him back to life. He may just give you all the love you need until the wave of sorrow has passed. Then He helps you to realize that what you've endured has made your inner warrior woman stronger and even more dedicated to Him.

When the walls close in, turn to Jesus. Know that He sees you and feels compassion toward you. Crawl up onto His lap and receive the comfort He offers, knowing He alone can transform your sorrow and loss into strength and courage.

THANK YOU, LORD, FOR SEEING ME, FOR BEING THERE,
FOR HOLDING ME CLOSE THROUGH EVERYTHING.

A LOAD OFF

*"Come to me. Get away with me and you'll recover your life.
I'll show you how to take a real rest. Walk with me and work
with me—watch how I do it. Learn the unforced rhythms of
grace. I won't lay anything heavy or ill-fitting on you. Keep
company with me and you'll learn to live freely and lightly."*

MATTHEW 11:28–30 MSG

Many days we may find ourselves caught up in this world, zooming
from one task to another to get the laundry done, clean the house,
pick up the kids, drive to work, feed the family, get to church, etc.,
etc. Yet during each day there may be in the back of our minds a
worry—about whether we're raising the kids right, if we'll get our
work done on time, if we perhaps voted for the wrong candidate, if
our checking account can get us through till payday. Our thoughts
are endless. And with each negative one, a burden is added to our
shoulders.

It's time to take the time to sit at Jesus' feet. To rest in His
presence. To allow Him to take the load off. Those are the moments
when our warrior woman is not suppressed but comes to life, now
free of the frets from daily demands, ready once more to enter God
territory and do the work He has called us to do, freely and lightly.

*LORD, SITTING AT YOUR FEET,
MY BURDENS SLIDE OFF MY SHOULDERS.
MY WARRIOR WOMAN AWAKENS.*

TRUST FOR ALL

God strengthens the weary and gives vitality to those
worn down by age and care. Young people will get tired;
strapping young men will stumble and fall. But those who
trust in the Eternal One will regain their strength. They will
soar on wings as eagles. They will run—never winded,
never weary. They will walk—never tired, never faint.
Isaiah 40:29–31 voice

When your inner warrior woman is weak and can't seem to find her feet, consider what you're putting your faith in, what you're trusting to get you through the days and nights that comprise your life.

Nothing else but God is your source of strength. If you're tired, He'll refresh and rejuvenate you. Whether you're a young woman or one of mature years, you will become weary if you do not trust in God for all things. For only when He has your complete and enduring trust regarding all things—such as provision, protection, and so on—will you find the strength that will help you to soar like an eagle, to walk and run for miles, and never tire, never grow faint, never become winded.

Every moment of your day and night, trust your Creator. And watch your warrior woman grow strong, allowing nothing to frighten or shake her.

LORD, I AM WEARY. FILL MY INNER
WARRIOR WITH ALL THE STRENGTH I
NEED AS I GROW MY TRUST IN YOU!

ENCOURAGED AND STRENGTHENED

*David was greatly distressed, for the men spoke of
stoning him because the souls of them all were bitterly
grieved, each man for his sons and daughters. But David
encouraged and strengthened himself in the Lord his God.*

1 SAMUEL 30:6 AMPC

David and his men had been off warring. By the time they came
home to Ziklag, they saw a devastating sight. The Amalekites had
burned down their town and carried away their wives, sons, and
daughters.

All the men, including David, were in anguish. "They cried out
and wept aloud until they could weep no more" (1 Samuel 30:4
VOICE). Things got even uglier as David's men, wild with grief, began
to talk about killing him.

Where did David turn? To God. He prayed to Him, entrusting
his troubles, himself, his family, and his future to God. For in Him
alone was David's source of strength and courage. But he didn't
stop there. He asked God what to do. And God answered.

In the end, David and his men not only recovered all that had
been taken but brought back the Amalekites' own flocks and herds.

When faced with loss, allow yourself to grieve. But then take
courage from God, asking Him, "What would You have me do next?"

*YOU KNOW MY TROUBLES, LORD. NOW I NEED
YOUR COURAGE, STRENGTH, AND WISDOM AS I
ASK, "WHAT WOULD YOU HAVE ME DO NEXT?"*

YOUR PERSONAL GOD

*"Don't be afraid, I've redeemed you. I've called your name.
You're mine. When you're in over your head, I'll be there
with you. When you're in rough waters, you will not go
down. When you're between a rock and a hard place,
it won't be a dead end—because I am GOD, your
personal God, the Holy of Israel, your Savior."*
ISAIAH 43:1–3 MSG

When fear comes knocking at your door—and it will—
remember you're not your own. You're not in charge. You have a
heavenly Father who has redeemed you. He called you to this life,
this way you're walking.

So stop trying to run your own life. Put yourself in the
hands of your Creator, God Almighty. Know that when the
stormy waves begin to crash over your head, you won't go
under because He's holding you up. When you, like the Israelites at the Red Sea, find yourself between a rock and a
hard place, God will help you find your way out. He will
divide the waters so that you will have an escape route.

You, warrior woman, have a personal God, one you can call
on at any time. His number is never unlisted. And He's only a
whisper away.

WHEN I FEEL AS IF I'M DROWNING, WHEN I'M
BETWEEN A ROCK AND A HARD PLACE, LORD,
I WILL NOT PANIC OR FEAR. FOR YOU ARE WITH
ME. YOU HAVE AND WILL CONTINUE TO SAVE
ME. FOR YOU ARE MY PERSONAL GOD.

NOTHING TOO HARD

And the Lord asked Abraham, Why did Sarah laugh, saying,
Shall I really bear a child when I am so old? Is anything
too hard or too wonderful for the Lord? At the appointed
time, when the season [for her delivery] comes around,
I will return to you and Sarah shall have borne a son.
GENESIS 18:13–14 AMPC

There may be a part of you that has trouble seeing yourself as a warrior woman. That's because "you are seeing things merely from a human point of view, not from God's" (Matthew 16:23 NLT).

Sarah, Abraham's wife, had the same problem. God, while visiting Abraham, told him that Sarah would have a son within the next year. Sarah, overhearing this seemingly outrageous statement, laughed. She said to herself, "How could a worn-out woman like me enjoy such pleasure, especially when my master—my husband—is also so old?" (Genesis 18:12 NLT). But it happened. God was true to His word.

Whenever you start to doubt what God can do in and through you, remember that nothing is too hard for Him. Doing so will help you to see things from God's perspective, envisioning that anything and everything is possible.

> *LORD, WHEN I BEGIN TO DOUBT THAT I AM*
> *A WARRIOR WOMAN, HELP ME REMEMBER*
> *THAT NOTHING IS TOO HARD FOR YOU!*

THE SPIRITUAL VIEW

David spoke to the men who were standing with him:
"What will be done for the man who kills that Philistine
and removes this disgrace from Israel? Just who
is this uncircumcised Philistine that he should
defy the armies of the living God?"

1 SAMUEL 17:26 HCSB

King Saul had arrayed his army of Israelites against the forces of the Philistines, separated by the valley of Elah. Every morning and evening the giant Philistine Goliath came out to taunt the Israelites, daring them to send someone to fight him. But, shocked and frightened, neither Saul nor anyone in his army was brave enough to take him up on his offer.

And then came the young David, sent by his father to take provisions to his older brothers who were out on the battlefield. Standing in the valley of Elah with the Israelites, David heard Goliath's challenge. Immediately taking the spiritual view of things, the courageous David asked, "What is the reward for removing this insult from Israel by killing this man? No uncircumcised Philistine can get away with taunting the armies of the living God!" (1 Samuel 17:26 VOICE).

When challenged, don't retreat in fear. Instead, take the spiritual view of things and remember that no one can defeat a warrior of God's force for good.

LORD, HELP ME TO SEE EVERY CHALLENGE
FROM YOUR STANDPOINT AND TO VENTURE
ON FROM THERE IN FAITH.

TURN AWAY

*Now Eliab his eldest brother heard what he said to the men;
and Eliab's anger was kindled against David. . . . And
David said, What have I done now? Was it not a harmless
question? And David turned away from Eliab.*

1 SAMUEL 17:28–30 AMPC

David had made known his position, how he saw the challenge by Goliath as an affront to God. He knew that God would not let this insult rest without taking some action. As David continued to ask others in the crowd what would be done for the man who slayed the giant, his brother Eliab began to get angry. He claimed that David had some agenda, that he should be home taking care of the sheep, that he'd come to the battlefield out of curiosity, nothing more. David simply turned away from Eliab.

As a warrior woman for God, follow David's example. Don't let those who accuse you of having a hidden agenda keep you from battling for God and good. Don't let them think you're crazy for seeing things from God's point of view. When others try to keep you from standing up for God, simply and gently turn away from them, ignoring their accusations and suppositions. Stand firm, undaunted by the opinions of others, with courage and strength, knowing the Lord is beside you, helping you every step of the way.

*IN YOUR POWER, LORD, I WILL IGNORE
THE NAYSAYERS AND STAND WITH YOU.*

SOURCE OF POWER

*The Lord Who delivered me out of the paw of the
lion and out of the paw of the bear, He will deliver
me out of the hand of this Philistine. And Saul
said to David, Go, and the Lord be with you!*

1 SAMUEL 17:37 AMPC

Word about David's eagerness and confidence in battling the giant Goliath made its way to King Saul's ears. So the shepherd boy was delivered to him. David reiterated his desire to fight, telling Saul to his face, "Don't let anyone be frightened because of that man. I am your servant, and I will go and fight with him" (1 Samuel 17:32 VOICE).

Saul thought the boy's statement ridiculous. After all, Goliath had been a warrior since he was a child. He told David, "You lack age and experience" (1 Samuel 17:33 VOICE).

Yet David was determined. He explained to the king how whenever a lion or bear attacked his lambs, he would kill it, just as he would this Philistine. David was confident that the God who'd saved him in those face-offs would do so again.

David's faith in God was stronger than the caustic remarks of his brother and the discouraging remarks of his king. May your faith be just as strong, opening new sources of power so that you too can battle giants.

*STRENGTHEN MY FAITH IN YOU, LORD, SO THAT I CAN
TAP INTO YOUR INFINITE STRENGTH AND POWER.*

CONFIDENCE IN GOD ALONE

So he removed every bit of Saul's armor. He would fight the Philistine as he had fought those lions and bears. He took his staff in his hand and went to the stream to choose five smooth stones.

1 SAMUEL 17:39–40 VOICE

The king was willing to allow David to fight Goliath. But he insisted David be outfitted in Saul's own armor, giving the boy a bronze helmet, a coat of mail, and a sword. But David could barely move in the heavy, restrictive gear.

David told Saul, "I'm not used to these things. How can I attack an enemy when I can't even walk?" (1 Samuel 17:39 VOICE). Determined to fight in his usual garb, David removed the helmet, mail, and sword. He armed himself with his shepherd's staff and chose five smooth stones from the brook and put them into his pouch. Sling in hand, he faced the Philistine.

David needed no other protection than God's. He was ready to fight the giant and conquer him in faith, his confidence in God alone, assured that the Lord would be with him and give him victory.

Know that God will give you the victory when your faith is placed in Him alone.

MAY I, LORD, TRUST IN NO ONE AND NOTHING BUT YOU TO GIVE ME THE STRENGTH AND COURAGE TO STAND UP TO GIANTS.

THE BATTLE IS GOD'S

*Then said David to the Philistine, You come to me with
a sword, a spear, and a javelin, but I come to you in the
name of the Lord of hosts. . . . And all this assembly shall
know that the Lord saves not with sword and spear; for the
battle is the Lord's, and He will give you into our hands.*

1 SAMUEL 17:45, 47 AMPC

David, with nothing more than a sling, staff, and stones, faced the
giant Goliath who was armored to the hilt!

After Goliath taunted him and cursed him, threatening to
feed his flesh to the birds and wild animals, David made it clear
that he had come "armed with the name of the Eternal One, the
Commander of heavenly armies" (1 Samuel 17:45 VOICE), and that
God would be the victor in this battle. And He was! For with God
on his side and armed with His power, David slew the giant with
merely a sling and a stone.

You, warrior woman, need only be equipped with faith to defeat
the giants in your life, to face the challenges that stand before you.
Walking with and in God, allow Him to fight all battles through you.
He will remove any obstacles that stand in your way.

*THANK YOU, LORD, FOR THE VICTORY
YOU GIVE IN ALL AREAS OF MY LIFE!*

RESOLVE TO SEEK GOD

People came and told Jehoshaphat, "A vast number from
beyond the Dead Sea and from Edom has come to fight against
you; they are already in Hazazon-tamar" (that is, En-gedi).
Jehoshaphat was afraid, and he resolved to seek the LORD.

2 CHRONICLES 20:2–3 HCSB

King Jehoshaphat had just "solidified his throne by fortify-
ing the nation and appointing regional judges" (2 Chronicles
20:1 VOICE) when "the Moabites and Ammonites, together
with some of the Meunites, came to fight against [him]" (2 Chronicles
20:1 HCSB). And he became afraid. So he determined to seek God.

When you have done all you can to ensure the safety of your
life and those you love, you may think you're home free. But often-
times you'll find that something comes along to disrupt and perhaps
destroy all your efforts. That's when you must resolve to seek God.
For only He can provide you with the strength and courage to
endure whatever has come against you.

God would not have you attempt to do anything without His
power and presence at your side, without His wisdom to help you
through, without His shield to keep you safe in His arms.

WHEN TROUBLE COMES, LORD, MAY MY FIRST ACT
BE NOT TO BE OVERCOME BY FEAR BUT TO RESOLVE
TO SEEK YOU AND ALL YOU HAVE TO OFFER.

POWER IN GOD'S HANDS

Yahweh, the God of our ancestors, are You not the God who is in heaven, and do You not rule over all the kingdoms of the nations? Power and might are in Your hand, and no one can stand against You. Are You not our God who drove out the inhabitants of this land before Your people Israel and who gave it forever to the descendants of Abraham Your friend?

2 CHRONICLES 20:6–7 HCSB

When you seek God in prayer—public or private—take some time to remember and proclaim who God is and what He has done in the past, whether in your own life or in His history. Doing so will remind you that He is the God of all who have gone before you. He is the God who holds all power and might in His hands. That *no one* can stand against Him—no matter how big or strong they may look in your human eyes. Remember all that God, your friend, has given you, because you are His princess, His daughter, the one He has saved and will always save.

AS I SEEK YOU, LORD, MAY I REMIND YOU AND MYSELF, AND PROCLAIM ALL OF YOUR AMAZING POWER IN THE PAST AND ALL THE TIMES YOU HAVE SAVED YOUR BELOVED ONES.

PRAYER ANYWHERE

"Your people settled here and built this Temple to honor
your name. They said, 'Whenever we are faced with any
calamity such as war, plague, or famine, we can come
to stand in your presence before this Temple where
your name is honored. We can cry out to you to
save us, and you will hear us and rescue us.' "

2 CHRONICLES 20:8–9 NLT

No matter where you are, no matter how powerful the force that comes against you, remember that when you're faced with calamity and cry out to the Lord, He will hear your prayer. And He will rescue you. Knowing this truth, this fact, can keep you standing firm in whatever challenges come before you.

Know also that you can pray anywhere and at any time, and God will hear you. Whether you're standing in a classroom full of kids, shopping at the grocery store, heading down the highway, making a presentation, getting ready for a meeting, doing the laundry, washing your hair, or driving to work, God will hear you. He will respond. He will answer you, protect you, help you.

Today, pray to the one whose ears are always open day and night. Then allow your confidence and courage to grow as you stand ready to hear His answer and do whatever He asks you to do.

THANK YOU, LORD, FOR HEARING AND
ANSWERING MY PRAYER FROM ANYWHERE.

EYES ON GOD

We have no might to stand against this great
company that is coming against us. We do not
know what to do, but our eyes are upon You.
2 Chronicles 20:12 AMPC

Jehoshaphat was a king, yet he remained humble. He had requested that his people gather in the almighty God's house. Then, standing before them in prayer, he admitted to his God that he and his people were "powerless against this mighty army that is about to attack" (2 Chronicles 20:12 NLT). He also admitted that none of them had any idea what to do. The only thing they had going for them was God. And all eyes were on Him.

There may be situations in which you too realize that you don't have the power to stand against whatever has come encroaching upon your borders. And that you have no idea what to do. But along with that, you must remember that, as a warrior woman, you have God in your corner. And all you have to do is keep your eyes on God.

If only Peter, when Jesus had invited him to walk on the water with Him, had kept his eyes on Jesus instead of on the wind and treacherous waters, he never would have begun to sink beneath the waves in fear (Matthew 14:22–33)!

Keep your eyes on God, knowing He's the only resource you ever need!

LORD, I'M PUTTING MY FAITH BEFORE MY
FEAR BY KEEPING MY EYES ON YOU!

WHOSE BATTLE IS WHOSE?

Listen to me, all Judah, citizens of Jerusalem,
and King Jehoshaphat. The Eternal has responded to
your pleading: "Do not fear or worry about this army.
The battle is not yours to fight; it is the True God's."

2 CHRONICLES 20:15 VOICE

Jehoshaphat had prayed to the almighty God. All of Judah—men, women, and children—were awaiting God's response. And then God's Spirit descended on Jahaziel, a Levitical singer. Through him, God told the tense crowd and its king that God had heard their prayer. And God responded, telling them they need not fear the massive army of mortals that had come to overtake them—because this battle wasn't theirs but God's.

Then God, through Jahaziel, got into the specifics: "Tomorrow, they will travel through the ascent of Ziz. Meet them at the end of valley before the wilderness of Jeruel. There, I will be watching. Stand and watch, but do not fight the battle. There, you will watch the Eternal save you" (2 Chronicles 20:16–17 VOICE).

As a warrior woman, you must do these three things when a threat comes against you: be humble, appeal to God for help, and wait for His answer. So patience, woman. God hears. He will answer. And He'll let you know whose battle is whose.

HELP ME, LORD, TO COME TO YOU BEFORE I
MAKE ONE MOVE ON THE BATTLEFIELD.

COMPLETE TRUST

[Jahaziel]: Do not fear or worry. Tomorrow, face the army and trust that the Eternal is with you. Jehoshaphat bowed his head low, and all the assembly fell prostrate before the Eternal and worshiped Him with reverence. They trusted the Lord completely.

2 CHRONICLES 20:17–18 VOICE

Two times God, speaking through Jahaziel, told the people not to worry or fear. Two times He told the people that the battle was not theirs but His. God also made it clear to the people that they were to watch God saving them. Finally, the Lord asked them to trust that He was with them. And as they bowed before God and worshipped Him, their trust in Him was complete.

There is no victory for any warrior woman if trust in God is absent. For one thing, chances are she will come up with her own battle plan, "just in case God has got it wrong or didn't consider every aspect of the problem." Or she will cave in to worry and fear because she doubts that God can handle the situation.

Remember that Father God always knows best. Remember Him telling you, "My intentions are not always yours, and I do not go about things as you do. My thoughts and My ways are above and beyond you, just as heaven is far from your reach here on earth" (Isaiah 55:8–9 VOICE).

LORD, HELP ME TRUST YOU COMPLETELY, REMEMBERING YOU HAVE THE GREATER PLAN AND WISDOM!

TRUST 101

Early the next morning they went out to the wilderness of Tekoa.
There Jehoshaphat's message to Judah was not about courage
in battle. . . . Listen to me, Judah and inhabitants of Jerusalem.
Trust in the Eternal One, your True God, not in your own
abilities, and you will be supported. Put your trust in His words
that you heard through the prophets, and we will succeed.

2 CHRONICLES 20:20 VOICE

We pray to God for help and then assume that the only way we'll be successful is by taking care of the difficulty ourselves. We're like a child who has asked her daddy for help, and before he can even give her advice or begin to put his plan into place, she's toddled off on her own, determined to solve the problem, trusting in her own feeble abilities instead of his!

Being a warrior woman means you have to trust God—for everything. You must trust in His Word, for only then will you experience success.

In this incident, the people were not to fight but simply to watch God work. Their attempts to handle the situation would only put them in harm's way.

In what areas of your life do you need to stand firm and watch God do His thing? Do you trust Him enough to leave everything—the battle *and* the results—in His hands?

> ENTER ME, LORD, IN THE SCHOOL OF TRUST
> SO THAT I COUNT ON YOU MORE THAN ON
> MYSELF AND MY OWN ABILITIES.

PRAISE AMAZES!

*As they sang and praised, the Eternal was ready to cause
great confusion in battle for the men from Ammon, Moab,
and Mount Seir (in Edom) who had come to attack Judah.
They were utterly defeated, turning on one another.*

2 CHRONICLES 20:22 VOICE

After telling the people to trust in God and His Word instead of in themselves, "Jehoshaphat asked those who sang to the Eternal to lead the army and praise His magnificence and holiness," and the choir started singing, "Give thanks to the Eternal because His loyal love is forever!" (2 Chronicles 20:21 VOICE).

As soon as the people sang and praised God, He caused confusion in the enemy army encampments. They turned on and killed one another! No one escaped the slaughter. All that was left for Jehoshaphat and his people was to pick up the spoils left behind, including the fallen soldiers' valuables and their many livestock. And it took them three days to do it! On the fourth day, they named the valley where all this took place the Valley of Blessing.

Take note, warrior woman. Your praise to God can do amazing things! And if you count on Him alone, He will give you victory in the valley of blessing!

*THANK YOU, LORD, FOR ALL THE LOVE YOU HAVE FOR
YOUR PEOPLE. I THANK YOU ALONE FOR EVERYTHING!
TO YOU BELONG ALL PRAISE AND GLORY!*

CREDIT WHERE CREDIT IS DUE

Then all the men returned to Jerusalem, with Jehoshaphat
leading them, overjoyed that the LORD had given them
victory over their enemies. They marched into Jerusalem
to the music of harps, lyres, and trumpets, and
they proceeded to the Temple of the LORD.

2 CHRONICLES 20:27–28 NLT

When the men returned from the Valley of Blessing to Jerusalem, they were filled with joy! And they expressed it to the hilt! With their king leading them, they marched into the city, playing their music, and paraded all the way to and into the house of God.

Consider the things that led to this celebration. King Jehoshaphat's humility and faith, His seeking God for help, admitting he himself didn't know what to do. His and the people's complete trust in the Lord and His Word. Their fortitude to stand firm, to praise God and allow Him to do His work, to bring them victory. And the cherry on top? Giving credit to God, the giver of blessings. These people had their priorities straight. Do you?

LORD, HELP ME TO KEEP MY PRIORITIES STRAIGHT.
TO BE HUMBLE, LOOKING TO YOU ALONE FOR HELP,
ADMITTING I DON'T KNOW WHAT TO DO. TO TRUST YOU
AND YOUR WORD. TO STAND AND WAIT FOR YOU TO
BRING VICTORY WHEN YOU SAY THE BATTLE IS YOURS.
TO PRAISE YOU BEFORE THE BATTLE AND TO GIVE YOU
ALL THE CREDIT FOR THE BLESSINGS THAT FOLLOW.

A WOMAN OF MITES

A poor widow came by and dropped in two small coins
[or mites]. "I tell you the truth," Jesus said, "this poor
widow has given more than all the rest of them. For
they have given a tiny part of their surplus, but she,
poor as she is, has given everything she has."

LUKE 21:2–4 NLT

It may be that you are a tither, that you give an offering each week at church, money to help others who need it, to help the church to survive, maybe even enough to thrive! But what about *you*? What of *yourself* do you give over to God?

You may feel as if you have nothing to give the Lord. But every follower of God has at least two mites she can give Him: her soul and her body.

A giving woman is one who doesn't just keep taking from God, praying to Him only when she's in trouble or needs help. A giving woman offers herself up to Him in prayer each day, asking Him to make it clear to her what she can do for Him—not just what He can do for her.

You are a warrior woman with a lot to offer. Whether ill or well, poor or rich, disabled or healthy and strong in body, God can use you in many ways. Why not ask Him how today?

> I OFFER YOU MY SOUL AND BODY, LORD.
> WHAT CAN I DO FOR YOU? HOW MAY I
> SERVE YOU IN THE HOURS BEFORE ME?

GOD THE PROMISE KEEPER

The LORD kept his word and did for Sarah exactly
what he had promised. She became pregnant, and she
gave birth to a son for Abraham in his old age. This
happened at just the time God had said it would.

GENESIS 21:1–2 NLT

At one time, the aged Sarah had laughed when she'd heard God say that she and her "old man" (Abraham) would have a son when He returned in a year. But, as God had asked Abraham then, "Is anything too hard for the LORD?" (Genesis 18:14 NLT).

God can do anything! Even what you consider impossible! All that He promises you, even the seemingly impossible, will happen. God keeps His word! There are no ifs, ands, or buts about it. What He says is gospel!

That fact, that truth—that God keeps His word and His promises—is what can give warrior women the strength and courage they need to face anything! That assurance is what can give you the peace, the calm, the determination, the persistence, the hope, the comfort to live in and serve the almighty Lord of all!

WHAT A WONDERFUL FEELING, LORD,
KNOWING THAT YOU ALWAYS KEEP YOUR WORD
AND PROMISES. YOU ALONE ARE MY SOLID ROCK,
MY BELOVED, MY STRENGTHENER AND GUIDE.

LEANING ON GOD

Lean on, trust in, and be confident in the Lord with all your heart and mind and do not rely on your own insight or understanding. In all your ways know, recognize, and acknowledge Him, and He will direct and make straight and plain your paths.

PROVERBS 3:5–6 AMPC

Today's verses are ones that a warrior woman needs to take to heart, to write upon her mind. For by relying on your own wisdom and intuition, chances are very good that you'll stumble on the path if not meander off it completely.

God would have you rely on His Word in every aspect of your life. For that is where all truth and wisdom lie. And "happy (blessed, fortunate, enviable) is the man who finds skillful and godly Wisdom, and the man who gets understanding [drawing it forth from God's Word and life's experiences]" (Proverbs 3:13 AMPC).

Look for God when you read His Word. Take time to listen for His wisdom, and then to take that wisdom and offer up a prayer, seeking further insight into what He would have you say and do, where He would have you go.

Last, but most certainly not least, give God praise for all the ways He helps you, minute by minute, hour by hour, day by day, step-by-step.

I'M LEANING ON YOU, LORD, TRUSTING YOU WITH ALL MY HEART AND MIND. GUIDE ME IN YOUR WISDOM. MAKE MY PATHS STRAIGHT.

KEEPING GOD IN SIGHT

Never lose sight of God's wisdom and knowledge:
make decisions out of true wisdom, guard your
good sense, and they will be life to your soul
and fine jewelry around your neck.

PROVERBS 3:21–22 VOICE

Keeping God's wisdom and knowledge in sight will is a must for all warrior women. For doing so will "keep you safe on your way, and your feet will not stumble" (Proverbs 3:23 NLT); and "when you lie down, you will not be afraid. . .and your sleep will be pleasant" (Proverbs 3:24 HCSB). Not only that, but you will discover there is no reason to be afraid. "For the Eternal is always there to protect you. He will safeguard your each and every step" (Proverbs 3:26 VOICE).

One of the best things you can do for yourself is to ground yourself in God's Word by making it an integral part of your life. Begin each morning with the Word, whether that takes the form of reading a few chapters before your feet hit the floor or taking a verse, several verses, or maybe just a fragment of a verse, one that really speaks to your heart, writing it down, and memorizing it so that when it is needed, it will be there to calm you, strengthen you, and encourage you. Never leave home—or heart—without the Word!

LORD, LEAD ME TO WHAT YOU'D HAVE ME
LEARN IN THE WORD. HELP ME MAKE
IT PART OF MY LIFE, PART OF ME!

QUAKE AND SHAKE

Picture this: It's midnight. In the darkness of their cell, Paul and Silas—after surviving the severe beating—aren't moaning and groaning; they're praying and singing hymns to God. The prisoners in adjoining cells are wide awake, listening to them pray and sing.
ACTS 16:25 VOICE

While in Philippi, Paul and Silas exorcised a spirit from a slave girl, a spirit that enabled her to tell fortunes. Her owners became enraged when they realized they could no longer make money off her particular talent. So they dragged Paul and Silas before the authorities. A mob quickly formed, and the chief magistrates ordered the two men to be stripped, beaten, and imprisoned.

Yet even then, while being carefully guarded and their feet secured in stocks, Paul and Silas prayed and sang hymns of praise to God! The other prisoners were listening to them. Then the earth quaked, and the jail was shaken. All the doors of the prison opened, and all the prisoners' chains were loosed!

Prayer and praise are two of the biggest weapons that you, a warrior woman, can have in your holy arsenal. The practice of both will not only change the tough situation you may find yourself in but will also change you and the people's lives you touch, inside and out.

IT'S AMAZING HOW EFFECTIVE THE TOOLS OF
PRAYER AND PRAISE ARE, LORD. MAY I REPLACE
MY MOANING AND GROANING WITH THE POWERS
THAT MAKE THE WORLD QUAKE AND SHAKE!

DOORS AND HEARTS OPENED

They replied, "Believe in the Lord Jesus and you will be saved,
along with everyone in your household." And they shared the word
of the Lord with him and with all who lived in his household.

ACTS 16:31–32 NLT

Prayer and praise not only got Paul and Silas out of prison but also gave them the opportunity to share the Word with unbelievers.

After the earth quaked, the jail shook, prison doors opened, and chains fell off, the jailer was about to kill himself, for he thought all the prisoners had escaped. But Paul, in his compassion, "called out in a loud voice, 'Don't harm yourself, because all of us are here!'" (Acts 16:28 HCSB). The jailer then fell down before Paul and Silas, escorted them out, and asked how he could be saved. Paul told him simply to believe in the Lord Jesus. That night the jailer and everyone in his household believed and were baptized.

The next day, the magistrates, having discovered that Paul and Silas were Roman citizens, not only apologized to the two apostles but escorted them out of town!

When you come to God in prayer and praise, do it with your entire heart, strength, and mind. Then watch how He shakes up your situation, opening doors and hearts.

YOU, LORD, ARE AMAZING! I PRAY TO AND PRAISE YOU WITH MY ENTIRE BEING, HELPING TO MAKE A WAY TOWARD YOU OPENING DOORS AND HEARTS.

GOD OF SEEING

As a result of this encounter, Hagar decided to give the Eternal
One who had spoken to her a special name because He had seen
her in her misery. Hagar: I'm going to call You the God of Seeing
because in this place I have seen the One who watches over me.

GENESIS 16:13–14 VOICE

How comforting to know God doesn't just see us but watches
over us as well.

God had promised Sarah and Abraham that they, even in their
old age, would have a child. But as the years passed, the promise
hadn't come to fruition. So Sarah decided to give her servant Hagar
to her husband Abraham and gain a child in that way. This plan
worked—to a point. Hagar did become pregnant, but then she began
to treat Sarah with contempt. Sarah, in turn, began mistreating
Hagar to the point that Hagar ran away, into the wilderness, alone
and miserable.

The angel of the Lord found Hagar there. He shared with her
words of comfort, words that gave her the strength and courage
to go back to her master and mistress.

When you are feeling miserable and alone, know that God sees
you. He has words of comfort just for you, words that will give you
the strength and courage to go on—even to go back.

THANK YOU, LORD, FOR SEEING ME,
UNDERSTANDING ME, WATCHING OVER ME.
THANK YOU FOR THE WORDS OF COMFORT THAT
GIVE ME THE STRENGTH AND COURAGE TO CARRY ON.

SHARING THE JOY

Abraham was 100 years old when Isaac was born.
And Sarah declared, "God has brought me laughter.
All who hear about this will laugh with me. Who would
have said to Abraham that Sarah would nurse a baby?
Yet I have given Abraham a son in his old age!"

GENESIS 21:5–7 NLT

At one time, Sarah had laughed when she'd overheard God telling her husband Abraham that she and he would have a child (Genesis 18:12–15). But God reminded them both that nothing was too difficult for Him to accomplish.

Now, in their old age, Abraham and Sarah did indeed bring a child forth into this world. They gave him the name Isaac, which means "laughter," because this miracle gave both parents such joy! It was so contrary to the natural course of things.

When God does the seemingly impossible in your life, when He does something so contrary to nature that you realize it *must* be a miracle—whether that miracle be tiny or huge—laugh. And invite God to laugh with you, to share the joy. While you're at it, give Him all the thanks and praise that swells your heart. Doing so will boost you and God!

WHEN YOU DO SOMETHING AMAZING IN MY LIFE,
LORD, SOMETHING BEYOND ANYTHING I COULD
IMAGINE, MAY I REMEMBER TO SHARE THE JOY
WITH NOT JUST THE PEOPLE AROUND ME BUT MOST
ESPECIALLY WITH YOU, THE GIVER OF JOY!

LOOK UP

*God heard the boy crying, and the angel of God called
to Hagar from heaven, "Hagar, what's wrong? Do not be
afraid! God has heard the boy crying as he lies there. Go to
him and comfort him, for I will make a great nation from
his descendants." Then God opened Hagar's eyes.*

GENESIS 21:17–19 NLT

The first time Hagar was in the wilderness, she had run away. This time she'd been sent away because Ishmael (Abraham and Hagar's son) was teasing Isaac (Abraham and Sarah's son). Not only that, but Sarah didn't want Ishmael to share in her son's inheritance.

So in today's verses, we find Hagar and her son wandering in the wilderness and out of water. Hagar sets Ishmael in the shade of a bush, and she, about a bowshot away, sits down and weeps. So does Ishmael, and that's what attracts God's attention. Once again God is looking down, seeing the distressed, and offering words of comfort. Then He does something more. He opens Hagar's eyes. "She looked up from her grief and saw a well of water not far away" (Genesis 21:19 VOICE).

When we are too upset to find a solution or even pray for one, God sees, hears, comforts, and instructs us to look up from our grief, to look upon Him, with eyes and ears wide open, ready to receive.

*THANK YOU, LORD, FOR ALWAYS BEING THERE,
FOR SEEING ME, FOR HEARING ME IN A WORLD
THAT IS SOMETIMES TOO MUCH LIKE A WILDERNESS.*

PERPETUAL FOCUS

PERPETUALLY my focus takes me to the Eternal
because He will set me free from the traps laid for
me. . . . My gaze is fixed upon You, Eternal One,
my Lord; in You I find safety and protection.
PSALM 25:15, 141:8 VOICE

Are your eyes on God? Is your trust in Him? Do you look to Him alone to provide relief?

These are questions to ask yourself when you are in dire straits. For even when others may turn away from you, God never will. He has been there for you in the past. He is here with you in this very moment. And He will be with you in the future. But you won't see Him if you aren't looking. You won't find Him if you aren't seeking.

God does see what's happening in your life. But your relationship with Him cannot be one-sided. You must focus on Him as much as He is focused on you, watching to see what path you're taking, what you might need Him to provide.

Psalm 123:2 (HCSB) puts it this way: "Like a servant's eyes on his master's hand, like a servant girl's eyes on her mistress's hand, so our eyes are on the LORD our God until He shows us favor."

Today and every day, warrior woman, keep your focus on God, knowing He is your pathway to freedom, safety, and protection.

I LIFT MY EYES TO YOU, LORD, FIXING MY GAZE
ON THE ONE I CANNOT HELP BUT PRAISE.

GOD KNOWS BEST

*Joab (to Abshai): If the Arameans are too strong for
me, then you will help me; and if the Ammonites are too
strong for you, then I will help you. Be strong. Let us show
courage for the sake of our people and for the cities of
our God. May the Eternal do what He knows is best.*

1 CHRONICLES 19:12–13 VOICE

David sent Joab and his entire army of warriors to fight the Arameans
and Ammonites who were coming against Israel. When Joab saw
a battle line in front of and behind him, he divided up his troops
between him and his brother Abshai. The hope was that they could
help each other out as the battle progressed.

We too may sometimes find ourselves fighting battles from in
front and behind. But for the sake of God, we too can encourage
ourselves and others to be strong and courageous. Yet even more
important is the fact that regardless of what happens in the end,
we can trust that God will do what's best.

How freeing is that concept—that no matter how things turn
out, God has done, is doing, and will do what's best for us and
those we love!

So, take heart, woman. Stay strong. Do your best and leave
the results up to God!

THANK YOU, LORD, FOR THE FREEDOM OF THIS
TRUTH. I AIM TO LOOK TO YOU FOR ALL THE
COURAGE AND STRENGTH I NEED. I LEAVE
THE RESULTS IN YOUR CAPABLE HANDS!

GOING WITH GOD

*I prayed to the Eternal: "Eternal Lord, with Your outstretched
arm and Your enormous power You created the heavens
and the earth. Nothing is too difficult for You. . . . You are
the great and powerful God; the Eternal, Commander of
heavenly armies, is Your solemn name. Your instructions are
great, and Your actions are too wondrous for words."*
JEREMIAH 32:16–19 VOICE

You aren't just a lone warrior woman. You have a commander in
chief! His name is the Eternal Lord. So that battle you're trying to
fight, that war that you are waging against the darkness—do not
under any circumstances go it alone!

There's a reason God put us in a church family: so that we
can help each other along this road of life until we get to our true
home in heaven.

So when the going gets tough, go to your fellow warriors. Ask
them to pray with you or for you. Remind yourself (and them) that
God has the power to do anything. That nothing is too difficult
for the great I Am. That if you pray and if you listen, you will hear
God speak through His Word and His ways. Follow the instructions
your commander relays. And you cannot fail in His eyes, for you
are going with God.

LORD, YOU AND YOUR POWER ARE TOO WONDERFUL
FOR WORDS. NOTHING IS TOO DIFFICULT OR IMPOSSIBLE
FOR YOU. SO I COME IN PRAYER. . .READY TO LISTEN.

BELIEVE AND OBEY

From that day forward, Abraham called
that place, "The Eternal One will provide."
GENESIS 22:14 VOICE

Abraham and Sarah had one son: Isaac. And it was this son whom God called him to sacrifice (Genesis 22:12). So off Abraham went with two servants and Isaac in tow. He "traveled to the place God had told him about" (Genesis 22:3 VOICE). On the third day, Abraham told his servants to stay there with the donkey while he and Isaac went to the place where they would worship. He took up the wood for the offering and laid it on Isaac's shoulders. Then they walked off together, Abraham carrying the fire and a knife.

Along the way, Isaac, realizing they had the fire and wood, asked his father where the lamb for the offering was. Abraham told him God would provide it. Once they reached their destination, Abraham built an altar, arranged the wood, bound Isaac, and placed him on it. Just as he lifted the knife to kill his one and only son, God told him to stay his hand. For now He knew Abraham would obey Him.

Never doubt that God will provide whatever you need to do what He has called you to do. Your job is to believe, trust, and obey.

I DO TRUST YOU, LORD.
IT IS YOU WHOM I WILL OBEY.

THE TRUSTED SERVANT

*The Lord, the God of heaven, Who took me from my father's
house. . .Who spoke to me and swore to me, saying, To your
offspring I will give this land—He will send His Angel before you.*

GENESIS 24:7 AMPC

When Abraham was very old and had already buried Sarah, he
asked his most trusted servant, who some believe was Eliezer, to
find a wife for Isaac from among Abraham's own relatives in the
city of Nahor. Eliezer swore to do as his master required.

Gathering up camels and valuable gifts, he set off on his journey.
When he reached his destination, he stopped at a well just outside
the city. And he began to pray, "O Eternal One, God of my master
Abraham, please make me successful today" (Genesis 24:12 VOICE).
He asked that whichever girl offered him and his camels water would
be the woman God had chosen for Isaac's wife. Then "before he
could finish his prayer" (Genesis 24:15 VOICE), God answered it by
the appearance of Rebekah.

Warrior woman, you too are a trusted servant of God. As such,
when you are sent on a mission for your Master, be assured that
not only does His angel go ahead of you to clear the way but that
before your prayer is finished, it has been answered.

THANK YOU, LORD, FOR SENDING YOUR ANGEL
AHEAD OF ME TO MAKE MY PATH SMOOTH
AND FOR ANSWERING MY PRAYERS
BEFORE I'VE EVEN SAID, "AMEN."

PRAISE OPENS DOORS

At this the man bowed in worship before GOD and prayed,
"Blessed be GOD, God of my master Abraham: How generous
and true you've been to my master; you've held nothing back.
You led me right to the door of my master's brother!"
GENESIS 24:26–27 MSG

Abraham's servant questioned the girl who offered him and his camels water. When he discovered that she was a relative of Abraham's, one for whom he was searching, one for whom he'd prayed, he stopped in his tracks. Right then and there, Eliezer bowed down, worshipped, and prayed to God. For He had sent him, a lowly servant, the answer to his prayer.

When God answers prayers, it's time for celebration. It's time to acknowledge how far He has helped you, how He has held nothing back, how He has led you right to the door you've been seeking.

This servant's praises were obviously said aloud, for they sent Rebekah off running to her mother's house to tell everyone what had happened. When her brother Laban heard the news, he went to the well, found Abraham's servant still standing at the spring, and invited him home, saying, "I've got the house ready for you" (Genesis 24:31 MSG). Another door opened.

When you praise God for answered prayers, He is already working on another answer!

YOU AMAZE ME, LORD, WITH ALL YOU DO FOR
YOUR SERVANTS. LIKE ABRAHAM'S SERVANT,
I TOO PRAISE YOU FOR YOUR GENEROSITY!

GOD'S CLEAR PATH

*"This is undeniably from God. We have no say in the matter,
either yes or no. Rebekah is yours: Take her and go; let her
be the wife of your master's son, as God has made plain."*

GENESIS 24:50–51 MSG

Abraham's servant Eliezer told the family of Bethuel (Rebekah's father) his story. How he'd been sent to procure a wife for Isaac from the family of Abraham. How he'd prayed for a sign from God at the spring and Rebekah had been the answer to that prayer before he had finished it.

The ever-practical Eliezer said, "Now, tell me what you are going to do. If you plan to respond with a generous yes, tell me. But if not, tell me plainly so I can figure out what to do next" (Genesis 24:49 MSG). Laban and Bethuel admitted that God had made His answer clear. And because of that, they really had no say in the matter.

Some events in life are so obviously from God that you really have no decision to make. All you need to do is follow His lead. When you do, you'll be surprised at how quickly strength and courage swell within you and sweep you along on the path God has devised.

*WHEN YOU MAKE YOUR INTENTIONS FOR ME
CLEAR, LORD, HELP ME NOT TO PROTEST BUT
ALLOW MYSELF TO BE SWEPT ALONG ON THE
PATHWAY YOU HAVE PLACED BEFORE ME.*

PERSISTENCE OF THE LESS

When he heard that Jesus the Nazarene was passing by,
he began to cry out, "Son of David, Jesus! Mercy, have
mercy on me!" Many tried to hush him up, but he yelled
all the louder, "Son of David! Mercy, have mercy on me!"

MARK 10:47–48 MSG

Those considered "less" by society often have a hard time being heard. Such was the case of a blind beggar named Bartimaeus. Picking up on the sounds emitted by the parade of people following Jesus, Bartimaeus realized He was passing by.

Bartimaeus cried out for Jesus. He identified Him as the Son of David, recognizing Him as the coming Messiah. Bartimaeus asked for Jesus to have mercy on him, knowing He had healed others before him and confident He could and would heal him. Others tried to quiet Bartimaeus, but that only made him shout even louder!

Perhaps there have been times when you have tried to make yourself heard and others told you not to make a scene, to go back into that pigeonhole in which they have placed you.

You, warrior woman, are a daughter of God, the mighty King. You are a sister to Jesus. And you have the Holy Spirit residing within you. Don't let anyone dissuade you from turning to Jesus, from calling out for His help. Ignore those who would keep you quiet. Take up your courage and persist until your request has been granted.

LORD, I KNOW I HAVE VALUE IN
YOUR EYES. HEAR MY PRAYER.

ALL OFF

Jesus stopped in his tracks. "Call him over."
They called him. "It's your lucky day! Get up!
He's calling you to come!" Throwing off his coat,
he was on his feet at once and came to Jesus.
MARK 10:49–50 MSG

Imagine that! Bartimaeus' persistence paid off big-time! Because he'd yelled his request to Jesus, making himself heard over the crowd that was trying to silence him, Jesus stopped in His tracks. Then He requested that others call Bartimaeus over.

Those who had at first believed the blind beggar to be beneath them were telling Bartimaeus to get up and come to Jesus. For now, instead of being guided by their own prejudices and desires, they were aligned with Jesus' compassion and wishes.

And Bartimaeus responded. He immediately threw off his coat, rose to his feet, and ran to Jesus. He had no fear, no despondency, only the faith of a poor blind man driving him to Jesus.

God's warrior woman needs to have the same gumption and persistence in going to Jesus for help. She must bravely throw aside whatever is encumbering her from seeking Him and allow herself to be guided by faith, not sight, knowing that Jesus alone is the answer to all her desires.

> LORD, HELP ME THROW OFF ALL THAT
> IS KEEPING ME FROM SEEKING YOU OUT,
> FROM TELLING YOU MY HEART'S DESIRES,
> FROM SEEING WITH THE EYES OF FAITH.

COURAGE AND HOPE

"What do you want me to do for you?" Jesus asked.
"My Rabbi," the blind man said, "I want to see!" And Jesus
said to him, "Go, for your faith has healed you." Instantly
the man could see, and he followed Jesus down the road.

MARK 10:51–52 NLT

Bartimaeus was now before Jesus. And the Lord asked him a very important question: "What do you want Me to do for you?"

Suppose you were standing before Jesus. How would you respond to His question? Would you tell Him what you *think* He *wants* to hear? Would the answer be ready on your lips, or would you have to think about it? What have you been asking Him to do for you? What might you be afraid to ask Him to do?

Of course, Jesus already knows your desires. But He wants you to voice them. He wants you to stand before Him, all encumbrances aside, and tell Him what you truly want. All you need is courage and hope. Your faith will do the rest.

Today, run to your friend Jesus. Believe that He can give you all you desire. And then follow Him wherever He goes.

**LORD, GIVE ME THE COURAGE TO TELL YOU MY DEEPEST
DESIRES AND THE HOPE OF THEM BEING GRANTED.**

FAITH FELLS FEAR

When struck by fear, I let go, depending securely upon You
alone. In God—whose word I praise—in God I place my trust.
I shall not let fear come in, for what can measly men do to me?
PSALM 56:3–4 VOICE

It's okay to be afraid sometimes. It's a natural human reaction, part of the fight, flight, and freeze response, the way your body faces any perceived threat. The trick is not to stay there.

So, how do you get through those moments? By letting go of what your body is telling you and setting your mind and heart to the matter. Begin by remembering that God is on your side, always has and always will be. That He is surrounding you with a protective and impenetrable shield. That He is the rock you stand on—the one who gives you a firm foundation and all the power you need to fight any foe.

The more you think about God, the more of His Word you call up from your mind, the quicker the fear will dissipate. And before you know it, the calm and courage you need cover you like a soft blanket. And you begin to wonder why you were ever concerned in the first place.

WHEN STRUCK BY FEAR, LORD, HELP ME LET GO OF
IT AND REACH OUT FOR YOU, KNOWING THAT YOU
ARE MIGHTIER THAN ANYTHING ELSE THAT MAY
COME AGAINST ME AND REALIZING THAT FAITH
ALWAYS FELLS FIGHT, FLIGHT, AND FREEZE.

GOD'S SIDE

*"I pulled you in from all over the world, called you in from
every dark corner of the earth, telling you, 'You're my
servant, serving on my side. I've picked you. I haven't
dropped you.' Don't panic. I'm with you. There's no need
to fear for I'm your God. I'll give you strength. I'll help
you. I'll hold you steady, keep a firm grip on you."*

ISAIAH 41:9–10 MSG

Imagine: God picked you. You! *You!* He called your name, chose you, pulled you out of the recesses of darkness. He told you who you were: His servant, one who was picked for His team. One who He has not let fall—and never will.

Perhaps you have had some people in your life who chose you and then rejected you. Or forgot about you. Or abused you. Or dropped you. But God is not like people. He doesn't lie. He doesn't let go. He doesn't give up. And nothing in the world—visible or invisible—can ever conquer or eradicate Him. That means that you'll always be on the winning team!

So, warrior woman, remember who's coaching you—who calls you His. Playing on Jehovah's team means you need not fear anything because He's always around and He'll give you all the strength and help you'll ever need—on this side of heaven and beyond!

*THANK YOU, LORD, FOR CALLING ME UP
TO PLAY ON YOUR TEAM. IN YOU I FIND
MY STRENGTH, COURAGE, AND SELF.*

HEART-TO-HEART CONVERSATIONS

When I heard this, I sat down and wept. In fact, for days I mourned, fasted, and prayed to the God of heaven. . . . "O Lord, please hear my prayer! Listen to the prayers of those of us who delight in honoring you. Please grant me success today by making the king favorable to me. Put it into his heart to be kind to me."

NEHEMIAH 1:4, 11 NLT

Nehemiah was an exiled Jew living in Persia, a cupbearer to the king. A visiting relative told him how the Jews who'd escaped exile were doing back in Jerusalem. They were in trouble, for the wall of Jerusalem was reduced to a pile of rubble and its gates destroyed by fire.

This news distressed Nehemiah for several days. His prayers during that time of mourning were probably more like wails and groans than actual sentences. Then he pulled himself together and prayed a long prayer, asking for God to forgive the sins of His people and help them. At the end of Nehemiah's prayer, he asked God to give him courage and make the king's heart tender when he came before the king to ask permission to go to Jerusalem. That's exactly what Nehemiah needed to make this difficult conversation a success.

Remember that prayer not only changes your heart but the hearts of others.

LORD, I PRAY YOU WOULD SOFTEN THE HEART OF THE ONE I MUST SPEAK TO TODAY AND GIVE ME COURAGE TO APPROACH A DIFFICULT SUBJECT. MAY YOU GRANT OUR CONVERSATION SUCCESS.

SOS PRAYERS

The king then asked me, "So what do you want?" Praying under
my breath to the God-of-Heaven, I said, "If it please the king,
and if the king thinks well of me, send me to Judah, to the
city where my family is buried, so that I can rebuild it."
NEHEMIAH 2:4–5 MSG

There are those long prayers you pray in private. You know, "when
you pray, go into your private room, shut your door, and pray to
your Father who is in secret. And your Father who sees in secret
will reward you" (Matthew 6:6 HCSB). Those are the kind of prayers
Nehemiah had been praying after he'd heard the disturbing news
about the walls of Jerusalem having been destroyed.

Now he, a cupbearer to the king, had to appear before Artaxerxes
and ask for some time off. He'd already prayed for God to give him
courage and success for this conversation. Yet he was still filled with
fear because Artaxerxes noticed his sad countenance, something
that could never be tolerated in the royal's presence.

Nehemiah began explaining to King Artaxerxes why he was
sad. This was followed by the king asking what he wanted of him.
That's when Nehemiah sent up a quick SOS prayer to God, praying
it underneath his breath.

God hears all prayers, even those quick ones, as short as a
breath. When you need courage, favor, protection, anything—no
matter where or when—pray. God hears. He will answer.

LORD, HEAR MY PRAYER!

TRUE SOURCE

My True God had heard my prayers and
rested His hand of favor and love upon me.
The king gave me everything I asked for!
NEHEMIAH 2:8 VOICE

Nehemiah had asked God to give him the courage to talk to the king about getting some time off so that he could go to Jerusalem to repair the city wall. He'd also asked God to make the king's heart tender so that his request to the king would be granted.

As a result, not only was the time off granted, but Nehemiah asked for and was given letters from the king that would give him safety during travel. Moreover, the king gave Nehemiah a supply of timber for rebuilding the wall, beams of the temple fortress, and a house for himself. "The king even sent along a cavalry escort" (Nehemiah 2:9 MSG)!

Today's verse reveals that although it was the king who had given Nehemiah everything he'd asked for, the credit for this favor went to God—not Artaxerxes! It was *God* who'd heard Nehemiah's prayer and answered it, blessing him left and right.

All that you are, have, and dream to be is from God. Give Him alone the thanks! From Him alone draw all the strength, courage, and favor you need!

THANK YOU, LORD, FOR ANSWERING MY PRAYERS,
FOR BLESSING MY LIFE, FOR GIVING ME MY DREAMS,
FOR LOVING ME MORE THAN I CAN FATHOM!

DREAM PLANTINGS

I got up at night and took a few men with me. I didn't tell anyone
what my God had laid on my heart to do for Jerusalem. . . .
I inspected the walls of Jerusalem that had been broken
down and its gates that had been destroyed by fire.
NEHEMIAH 2:12–13 HCSB

God had planted a plan in Nehemiah's heart, a plan to rebuild the walls of Jerusalem. But in God's wisdom, Nehemiah wanted to inspect the walls alone, under cover at night, before he told anyone else his ideas. That way he could counter any opposition the Jews might give him because he'd know exactly what needed to be done before he presented his proposition.

When Nehemiah did present his plan to the Jews, he told them how the gracious hand of God was on him, supporting him, and how the king was also favorable to this idea. In response, the Jews said, " 'Let's start rebuilding,' and they were encouraged to do this good work" (Nehemiah 2:18 HCSB).

Perhaps God has planted a dream in your own heart. If so, you can be wise like Nehemiah, keeping it to yourself until you've investigated all the parameters and are ready and confident to share it with others. Soon they'll all be on your side, willing to help!

THANK YOU, LORD, FOR PLANTING A DREAM IN
MY HEART. GIVE ME THE WISDOM AND COURAGE
TO SHARE IT WHEN THE TIME IS RIGHT.

CORKING MOCKERS

I shot back, "The God-of-Heaven will make sure we succeed.
We're his servants and we're going to work, rebuilding. You
can stick to your own business. You get no say in this!"
NEHEMIAH 2:20 MSG

After Nehemiah shared his God-prompted dream and plans with the Jews, they were very excited to be a part of the operation. His words gave them encouragement and strength.

Yet when others heard about his plans and the Jews' reaction to it, a few other people—specifically "Sanballat the Horonite, Tobiah the Ammonite official, and Geshem the Arab" (Nehemiah 2:19 MSG)—laughed at Nehemiah and the Jews and mocked them. They considered what was happening a rebellion against King Artaxerxes of Persia.

Nehemiah and the Jews could have lost their courage and confidence and given up. Or just sneaked away and hid. Or said nothing. But Nehemiah had already prayed to God for courage, and it was continually granted. He knew who held their success in His hands—God did. And that they were doing His work.

When others try to mock you as you pursue the vision God has planted in your heart, tell them God will grant you success. And keep moving forward. God's got this! And He's got you too!

WHEN OTHERS MOCK ME, LORD, GIVE ME THE
CONFIDENCE I NEED TO KEEP GOING, TO KEEP
PURSUING YOUR PLAN. HELP ME REMEMBER THAT
YOU ARE THE SOURCE OF ALL MY DREAMS AND
VISIONS. AND THAT YOU WILL ENSURE MY SUCCESS!

IMPRINT GOD ON YOUR MIND

Do not be afraid of the enemy; [earnestly] remember the
Lord and imprint Him [on your minds]. . .and [take from
Him courage to] fight. . . . And when our enemies heard that
their plot was known to us and that God had frustrated their
purpose, we all returned to the wall, everyone to his work.
NEHEMIAH 4:14–15 AMPC

Many were plotting against the efforts of Nehemiah and his workers
to rebuild Jerusalem's walls. The enemy's aim was to join against
Jerusalem, "to injure and cause confusion and failure" (Nehemiah
4:8 AMPC). But their aim was frustrated, for the people prayed to
God and set up a twenty-four-hour watch (verse 9).

Nehemiah wisely set some armed men in places where the wall
was least protected. Then he gave the builders a pep talk, telling
them to let go of their fear of the enemy and imprint God upon their
minds. For He would give them the courage to do what needed
to be done. And God did indeed fight for them (Nehemiah 4:20).

When fear creeps into your heart, focus on God. Remember
who He is and what He has done in your life and down through
the ages. Draw upon His power, strength, and courage to help you
do what He has called you to do. And He will!

MY EYES AND MIND ARE ON YOU, LORD! FROM
YOU I DRAW ALL THE STRENGTH, COURAGE,
AND POWER I NEED TO DO YOUR WILL!

GOD AT WORK

Even with all that interference, the wall was soon finished. . . .
The work had been accomplished in 52 days. When our enemies
heard the work was complete and the surrounding nations
saw our wall, their confidence crumbled. Only one possible
conclusion could be drawn: it was not just our efforts that
had done this thing. God had been working alongside us.
NEHEMIAH 6:15–16 VOICE

God working alongside His people—what an unbeatable combination!

Even with all the subterfuge, distractions, threats, mocking, and ridicule they had received from their enemies, the Jews finally finished building the wall around the city of Jerusalem. And it only took fifty-two days! The only explanation was that God had been at work in this situation, in this dream, making Nehemiah's vision a reality.

When God plants a dream in your heart, He doesn't just walk away and let you try to manifest that dream by yourself. No! He is working right alongside you.

On those days when you get frustrated or feel like giving up, during those sleepless nights when fears creep into your mind and heart and threaten to overtake you, in those moments when you hear others mocking your efforts, remember that God is with you. He will give you all the power, creativity, resources, courage, and strength you need to finish the task.

LORD, THANK YOU FOR TRAVELING THIS DREAM
ROAD WITH ME, WORKING BY MY SIDE. BECAUSE
YOU ARE WITH ME, I KNOW WE'LL SUCCEED!

PERPETUAL PROVISION

The LORD is my shepherd; I have all that I need.
PSALM 23:1 NLT

It's as simple as that. God is your shepherd. Whatever you need today, He will provide. God can and will provide anything and everything you can imagine, including but not limited to rest, guidance, peace, strength, courage, protection, comfort, honor, goodness, love, and blessings unbounded. Even more importantly than all those provisions just listed is the blessing and power of His presence.

So, when that feeling of lack comes to pay a call, don't answer it. If it tries to leave a voice mail, delete it. Know that you are a daughter of *the* King and, as such, nothing will be denied you. All you need to do is ask and wait with expectation.

Today, live in the knowledge that you lack nothing. Not one thing. For God is holding it all out to you. His hand extends toward you, filled with more things than you could ever hope or imagine. A good shepherd takes care of his sheep. So you can rest assured and gain strength from the fact that all you need is either already in your hands or winging its way to you on a breath and a prayer.

THANK YOU, MY GOOD SHEPHERD, FOR GIVING ME ALL THAT I NEED—IN THIS WORLD AND THE NEXT.

REST, RECONCILIATION, AND RENEWAL

He lets me rest in green meadows; he leads me
beside peaceful streams. He renews my strength.
PSALM 23:2–3 NLT

God, our good shepherd, knows exactly what we sheep need. He knows we're not the brightest bulbs in the chandelier. So He leads us where we need to be. Sometimes that place is one of rest. A place where we can catch our breath, pull back from the world, remember whose we are and why we are here. A place where we can safely shut our eyes, knowing that we are being guarded day and night by the most powerful force in the universe.

Other times, the place He brings us to is beside quiet waters. There the soothing sound of the water running down a hill or across the field or amid a stony pathway lulls us away from the stress of daily living on earth and onto a heavenly cloud where we have not a care in the world.

Wherever we are, we know that when we're with the good shepherd, in His presence, we will find all the strength we need to continue following Him.

In this moment, enter God's presence. Rest in His peace. Allow His strength to restore you.

HERE I AM, SHEPHERD LORD, MY
PRESENCE MELDING INTO YOURS.

CONSTANT COMPANION

*He guides me along right paths, bringing honor to his
name. Even when I walk through the darkest valley,
I will not be afraid, for you are close beside me. Your
rod and your staff protect and comfort me.*

PSALM 23:3–4 NLT

You, little lamb, are never in danger. For your good shepherd is guiding you every step of the way. And because you are following Him, hot on His heels, obeying His every signal, you will bring honor to His name.

No matter whether the roads are smooth or stony, God will lead you. He'll make sure you don't stumble. If your leg gets caught in a bramble because you've wandered off, He'll immediately respond to your bleats for help, rescue you, and bring you back into the fold of His loving arms.

Even through the darkest times, the ones where you can find no illumination, you need not be afraid. For your shepherd is right there beside you. He has a rod to protect you from anything that may come against you. And He has a staff to get your attention, something to focus on, so that you'll stay on the right path.

If you ever feel lost, unsure, and afraid, seek out your shepherd. Get back on that pathway to peace and comfort.

LORD, CONTINUE TO GUIDE ME. MAKE MY PATH
CLEAR. HELP ME REMEMBER THAT YOU ARE ALWAYS
BESIDE ME AND THAT I NEVER NEED TO FEAR THE
DARKNESS BECAUSE YOU ARE THE LIGHT OF MY LIFE!

UNDER A BROOM TREE

*Elijah was afraid and fled for his life. He. . .went on
alone into the wilderness, traveling all day. He sat down
under a solitary broom tree and prayed that he might die.
"I have had enough, LORD," he said. "Take my life, for I
am no better than my ancestors who have already died."*

1 KINGS 19:3–4 NLT

Ever have one of those days when your courage and faith seem to be unreachable? When you are ready to give it all up—including your own life?

That's where we meet up with the prophet Elijah. He had earlier called down the power of God onto a water-soaked stone altar, where God's flames turned both the sacrifice and altar to ashes. He'd executed the false prophets of Baal. But a death threat from Queen Jezebel was the last straw and sent Elijah running for his life.

Now here he was. In the wilderness. Alone. Under a broom tree. Asking the Lord to sweep his life away.

We are only human. And when we see—through human eyes—that our efforts and the powerful workings of God have not changed hearts, we may feel like Elijah, ready to pack it in.

Yet even in those dark places, God ministers to us. Gently. Calmly. Wonderfully.

*IN THOSE DIFFICULT MOMENTS, LORD,
WHEN I WANT TO GIVE EVERYTHING UP,
COME TO ME. GENTLY. CALMLY. WONDERFULLY.*

GOD MEETS US

Then he lay down and slept under the broom tree.
Suddenly, an angel touched him. The angel told him,
"Get up and eat." Then he looked, and there at his head
was a loaf of bread baked over hot stones, and a jug
of water. So he ate and drank and lay down again.
1 KINGS 19:5–6 HCSB

Elijah—tired and worn down emotionally, physically, mentally, and spiritually—slept, partaking in one of nature's best remedies. But even though he was in the wilderness, having tried to lose himself, God had not left him.

An angel told Elijah to get up and eat a loaf of warm bread and drink from a jug of water. He did so and then fell back asleep until the angel woke him a second time, telling him to eat and drink once more—for the prophet would need sustenance to endure the journey ahead.

God knows exactly *what* we need and *when* we need it. He gives us time to catch up on our sleep so that we will be refreshed once more. He sends angels to minister to us. No matter how far we go into the wilderness, we can be sure that God will meet us there.

THANK YOU, LORD, FOR MEETING ME WHERE
I AM, LOVING ME AS I AM, AND SENDING
ANGELS TO HELP ME WHEREVER I AM.

FED ON GOD'S WORD

So he got up and ate and drank, and the food gave
him enough strength to travel forty days and forty
nights to Mount Sinai, the mountain of God. There
he came to a cave, where he spent the night.

1 KINGS 19:8–9 NLT

Moses was up on the mountain of God for forty days and forty nights, having taken no food up with him (Exodus 24:18; Deuteronomy 9:9). Jesus Himself was in the wilderness for the same amount of time (Matthew 4:2). And in between Moses and Jesus was Elijah, traveling for forty days and nights, the food the angel had served him giving him enough strength for the journey.

Perhaps Elijah needed this walk—to help him sort things out in his mind, to meditate on the Word, to engage in private talks with God to help him gain God's perspective, to help him walk off the frustration, fear, and despondency that had brought him into the wilderness in the first place. Whatever Elijah did along the way, he did so in the strength of divine food, perhaps so that he "might learn that man does not live on bread alone but on every word that comes from the mouth of the LORD" (Deuteronomy 8:3 HCSB).

To stave off the world's pressures, to de-stress, to get a new perspective, feed on God's Word. You'll be amazed at the strength you gain from it.

AS I TRAVEL THIS ROAD, LORD,
FEED ME WELL UPON YOUR WORD.

STILL SMALL VOICE

The LORD was not in the wind. After the wind there was an earthquake, but the LORD was not in the earthquake. And after the earthquake there was a fire, but the LORD was not in the fire. And after the fire there was the sound of a gentle whisper.

1 KINGS 19:11–12 NLT

God spoke to Elijah, and His first words were, "What are you doing here, Elijah?" (1 Kings 19:9 NLT). Elijah replied, "I've been working my heart out for the GOD-of-the-Angel-Armies. . . . The people of Israel have abandoned your covenant, destroyed the places of worship, and murdered your prophets. I'm the only one left, and now they're trying to kill me" (1 Kings 19:10 MSG).

God told Elijah to stand on the mountain where He would pass by. A wind rose up, but God wasn't in the wind, nor in the earthquake or fire that followed. But He was in the gentle whisper that came to Elijah and asked once more what he was doing there.

Elijah gave God the same response. He told the story from his perspective, that he was the only prophet left. But God told him to go back, that there were seven thousand prophets left in Israel besides Elijah.

When you need a new perspective, seek God. Listen for the gentle whisper of His voice. Then go with confidence and strength wherever He sends you.

*THANK YOU, LORD, FOR SPEAKING
TO ME IN A GENTLE WHISPER.*

SOLITARY PRAYER

*Immediately Jesus made the disciples get into the boat
and go on to the other side of the sea while He dismissed
the crowd. Then, after the crowd had gone, Jesus went up
to a mountaintop alone (as He had intended from the start).
As evening descended, He stood alone on the mountain, praying.*
MATTHEW 14:22–23 VOICE

Earlier on the day our scripture passage speaks of, Jesus had been told about His cousin John the Baptist being beheaded. He tried to get away by Himself then. He even took a "boat to a remote place to be alone" (Matthew 14:13 HCSB), but the crowds followed Him on foot. And as soon as He stepped onto the shore, Jesus saw all the people, took pity on them, and healed them. Then, as if that wasn't enough, He fed them—five thousand men, not to mention all the women and children—with only five loaves and two fish.

Finally, Jesus, knowing He needed time alone with God to recharge and refresh, did what He had intended to do from the start. He sent everyone away, including the disciples, walked up the mountain, and had one-on-one time with His Father.

Today, set your intention to be alone with God. If that means sending the kids, husband, friend, or roommate away, or just putting a DO NOT DISTURB sign on your door, do it. Soak in the refreshment and rejuvenation of solitary prayer.

*HERE I AM, LORD. IT'S YOU
AND ME. ALONE. LET'S TALK.*

QUICK TO COMFORT

*Meanwhile, the disciples were in trouble far away
from land, for a strong wind had risen, and they were
fighting heavy waves. About three o'clock in the morning
Jesus came toward them, walking on the water.*

MATTHEW 14:24–25 NLT

While Jesus was getting His alone time with God, His disciples were in the boat. They were doing what He'd asked them to do: cross to the other side of the lake. But soon they found themselves in trouble. The wind had picked up, and the waves were getting bigger and stronger.

So Jesus went out to them. Walking. On the water!

It was three o'clock in the morning, and the disciples, battling wind and waves as they struggled to stay afloat and alive, saw what they thought was a ghost coming toward them. It scared them to death. They shouted, "It's a ghost!" (Matthew 14:26 NLT). "But Jesus was quick to comfort them. 'Courage, it's me. Don't be afraid' " (Matthew 14:27 MSG).

"Quick to comfort." When you're in trouble, when the darkness has overwhelmed you, when you're struggling to make headway, when you're terrified beyond reason, remember: Jesus will be quick to comfort you! To bring you back to yourself, to the realization that you have nothing to fear because Jesus is here.

WHEN I'M STRUGGLING AND FRIGHTENED, LORD,
COME QUICKLY TO COMFORT ME, TO GIVE ME THE
CALM AND COURAGE I NEED TO CARRY ON.

THAT SINKING FEELING

Jumping out of the boat, Peter walked on the water to Jesus.
But when he looked down at the waves churning beneath his
feet, he lost his nerve and started to sink. He cried, "Master,
save me!" Jesus didn't hesitate. He reached down and grabbed
his hand. Then he said, "Faint-heart, what got into you?"
MATTHEW 14:29–31 MSG

Assured that walking on the water was no ghost but Jesus, Peter boldly said, "Master, if it's really you, call me to come to you on the water" (Matthew 14:28 MSG). So Jesus did, telling Peter to "come ahead" (Matthew 14:29 MSG).

And Peter did! He walked on water to Jesus! How thrilling that must have been! Peter was on a real high. And then he looked away from Jesus. He saw the wind churning up the sea beneath his feet. His courage waned and fear came charging in. He called out for Jesus to save him.

Once again, Jesus was quick to the rescue, grabbing Peter's hand to keep him from sinking. Together they climbed into the boat.

When the wind begins to wail and the waves overwhelm, consider what you're focusing on. For it's that steady stare at Jesus that will keep you clear of that sinking feeling.

HELP, LORD! HELP ME FOCUS MY EYES ON YOU, TO BE
EVER CONSCIOUS OF YOUR PRESENCE, TO KNOW THAT
I NEED NOT FEAR BECAUSE YOU ARE RIGHT BESIDE
ME, READY TO SAVE AT A MOMENT'S NOTICE.

TRUE FOR YOU

*I am with you and will keep (watch over you with care,
take notice of) you wherever you may go. . .for I will not
leave you until I have done all of which I have told you.*
GENESIS 28:15 AMPC

Jacob had already gained his older brother Esau's inheritance by trading him a bowl of stew for it. And now Jacob and his mother tricked his father, Isaac, into blessing him instead of Esau. At this point, Esau was ready to kill Jacob.

Overhearing Esau's threat to her favorite son, Rebekah talked Jacob into leaving home and going to her brother Laban in Haran to find himself a wife. On his way, Jacob stopped to sleep in a certain place. He dreamed of a ladder from earth going up into heaven. Angels of God were going up and down that ladder, and God was at the top.

Then the Lord stood over Jacob and told him that He was with him and would watch over him wherever he went—that He'd be with him until He had done all He had promised him.

Feed your inner warrior woman on these promises. Allow them to fill you with all the comfort, strength, and courage you need to face this day and all the days to come.

THANK YOU, LORD, FOR ALWAYS BEING WITH ME,
WATCHING OVER ME, AND BLESSING ME WHEREVER I GO.

CALLING THE NOBODIES

Take a good look, friends, at who you were when you got called into this life. I don't see many of "the brightest and the best" among you, not many influential, not many from high-society families. Isn't it obvious that God deliberately chose men and women that the culture overlooks and exploits and abuses, chose these "nobodies" to expose the hollow pretensions of the "somebodies"?

1 CORINTHIANS 1:26–28 MSG

In the time of the judges, Midianites kept coming into Israel, raiding the crops and livestock. The people of God, hiding in caves and poverty stricken, cried out to the Lord for help.

So the angel of the Lord called a man named Gideon, who was "beating out wheat in the winepress so that the Midianites could not see what he was doing" (Judges 6:11 VOICE).

Gideon was basically a nobody. He admitted this to the angel, telling him, "My clan's the weakest in Manasseh and I'm the runt of the litter" (Judges 6:15 MSG).

Perhaps you view yourself as nothing special. You have no riches, no real position in society. But God doesn't care about any of that. He calls the "nobodies" on purpose, so that the "somebodies" would appear foolish. He raises up the weak to bring down the strong.

God can use you, warrior woman. Will you let Him?

LORD, I MAY NOT BE SPECIAL IN THE EYES OF THE WORLD, BUT I KNOW I'M SPECIAL TO YOU. I'M READY TO ANSWER YOUR CALL.

THE TRUE YOU

And the Angel of the Lord appeared to him and said to
him, The Lord is with you, you mighty man of [fearless]
courage. . . . Go in this your might, and you shall save
Israel from the hand of Midian. Have I not sent you?
JUDGES 6:12, 14 AMPC

The angel of God appeared to Gideon, saying, "The Lord is with you, you mighty man of [fearless] courage." That is how He addressed a man who was hiding from rampaging Midianites so they would not steal his wheat.

Gideon's first argument to the Lord's words was, "If You, God, are with us, why have all these bad things come to pass? What about all Your promises, miracles, blessings that were supposed to chase us? God brought us out of Egypt to this land and now He's gone, allowing the Midianites to overpower us."

Yet God sees Gideon as He sees you, a person He has come alongside, a mighty human of fearless courage. All you need to do is go in the power God gives you and do what He calls you to do.

God sees you as you truly are. Maybe it's time you see yourself as He does.

> HELP ME, LORD, TO SEE MYSELF AS YOU
> SEE ME, A WOMAN OF VALOR, ONE WHO
> CAN GO FORWARD IN YOUR POWER.

THE KEY TO VICTORY

"But Lord," Gideon replied, "how can I rescue Israel?
My clan is the weakest in the whole tribe of Manasseh,
and I am the least in my entire family!" The LORD said
to him, "I will be with you. And you will destroy the
Midianites as if you were fighting against one man."
JUDGES 6:15–16 NLT

Gideon tried to explain why he was not the man for the job, why he couldn't answer God's call. But God told him what each of us needs to remember, to know, to accept as truth: God is with us. And *because He is with us*, because He has chosen us, because He empowers us, we can do whatever He asks. And we can do it with and in the strength we never knew we possessed!

God's presence with you and His power within you is your key to victory—to doing what you might consider impossible.

Begin recognizing God's presence in your life. Feel His power growing within you with each word you read in the Bible. Allow His strength to build you up into the woman He has called. Let His courage surge through your body, mind, spirit, and soul, and you will become the warrior woman He already sees—the one He created you to be.

> BE WITH ME, LORD, AS I ALLOW YOU
> TO GROW ME INTO THE WARRIOR
> WOMAN YOU CREATED ME TO BE.

OPEN UP

Who is the King of glory? The LORD, strong and mighty;
the LORD, invincible in battle. Open up, ancient gates!
Open up, ancient doors, and let the King of glory enter.
PSALM 24:8–9 NLT

God has created you to be a warrior woman. He calls you into His presence, ready to be filled with His power and might. But there are times when you seem shut off from Him.

Your relationship with God is not a one-way street. You're not just to read His Word and pray your piece and then walk away. You are to read and then take in His Word, allowing it to penetrate the innermost part of your heart, to become the marrow in your bones. When you pray, you're to speak your piece and then listen to God's response.

And when you need strength, courage, and power, you're not to pray and stay closed off to God's presence. Instead, you're to throw open those ancient gates, open up the doors of your mind, heart, spirit, and soul. You're to let God enter your innermost being and give Him control, helping you to do the impossible.

Today and every day, take time to open wide those doors and gates. Let God enter in and overflow your warrior woman with all the strength and courage she needs.

LORD, I COME TO YOU, OPENING MYSELF TO YOUR PRESENCE. FILL ME WITH YOUR STRENGTH AND MIGHT, TODAY AND EVERY DAY.

THE REFUGE OF THE LORD'S WINGS

"How often I have wanted to gather your children
together as a hen protects her chicks beneath
her wings, but you wouldn't let me."

MATTHEW 23:37 NLT

Jesus longs for you to come to Him. His constant desire is for you to seek Him for protection, love, and grace. But how often do you turn away or refuse to acknowledge His presence?

In Psalm 57:1 (AMPC), David writes, "Be merciful and gracious to me, O God, be merciful and gracious to me, for my soul takes refuge and finds shelter and confidence in You; yes, in the shadow of Your wings will I take refuge and be confident until calamities and destructive storms are passed." Jesus has already granted you that grace and mercy, the calm and security you will find in Him. If you would just come. . . If you would run to Him. . . If you would hide yourself there until the difficult times pass by.

Ruth did it. She, with her mother-in-law, Naomi, walked from Moab to Bethlehem, where Ruth vowed that Naomi's God would be her God. And her future husband, Boaz, commended Ruth, saying, "May the LORD, the God of Israel, under whose wings you have come to take refuge, reward you fully for what you have done" (Ruth 2:12 NLT).

Jesus is waiting. Allow Him to gather you beneath His wings.

I COME TO YOU, LORD, NEEDING AND
WANTING TO TAKE REFUGE IN YOU.

ROCK STEADY

My words are always true and always here
with you. Heaven and earth will pass away,
but My words will never pass away.
MATTHEW 24:35 VOICE

You can count on few things in this life. There will be times when your friends betray you. Or someone you love will not return that blessing. Or no one will show you compassion. Or someone you once counted on will fail you. Or a child will disappoint you.

Myriad things in this life are uncertain, temporary, ever changing. The one and only thing you *can* count on is God's Word.

When others abandon you or slip through the cracks of your life, when the glaciers begin to melt and the seas rise, when the stars fall from the sky, when one you have loved is no longer here, remember the one thing you can depend on never leaving your mind and heart: God's Word.

Build your house, your life, your spirit, your soul, your mind, your heart, your entire being on God's Word. Then you will have firm footing as you walk through this life and beyond.

I WILL BUILD MY HOUSE AND LIFE ON YOUR
WORD, LORD. IT MAKES ME ROCK STEADY.

TIME TO SNUGGLE

[I can feel] his left hand under my head
and his right hand embraces me!
SONG OF SOLOMON 2:6 AMPC

There are times when you need to go to God for courage, to take that next big leap of faith. There are times when you need His strength to lift up yourself and others. There are times when you need His power to overcome a challenge. And there are times when you just need to snuggle up to Him. That's what today's verse invites you to do.

This is your moment to lay yourself down in that green meadow beside the meandering stream and feel His presence beside you. Here, in this place, allow your worries to fade into gray. Let your heart beat in rhythm with His. Feel His left hand under your heavy head. Allow His right hand to embrace you, pull you close. . .and rest.

Regardless of where you are or what you're doing, find that place beside God. Allow everything and everyone else to fall away. Let your burdens slide off your shoulders. Begin to breathe slowly and deeply, and drift away.

HERE I AM, LORD, ALLOWING MY MIND TO SLOW, MY
BURDENS TO FALL, MY HEART TO JOIN WITH YOURS.
I CAN FEEL YOUR LEFT HAND CRADLING MY HEAD AS
I LIE HERE IN YOUR PRESENCE, MY SPIRIT BECOMING
ONE WITH YOURS. AS YOUR RIGHT HAND EMBRACES
ME, YOUR PEACE FILLS MY SOUL. I AM YOURS.

WHERE YOU ARE

*Then Jacob awoke from his sleep and said, "Surely the
Lord is in this place, and I wasn't even aware of it!"*
GENESIS 28:16 NLT

No matter where you go, no matter the distance from your home, whether you are awake, asleep, or meditating, God is there with you. He's in the place where you reside.

Jacob was far away from home, on the run, and yet God was still with him. Just as He is with you.

The ladder Jacob dreamed of, the one that had angels climbing from earth to heaven and back again, reminds us that the Lord's messengers are continually going to and fro, watching over us, keeping tabs on us, making sure we are safe and sound.

You, like Jacob, may have situations in which you feel as if God is absent. Rest assured, He's there. Even when you aren't thinking about Him or haven't even asked for Him, God is with you.

Never forget that God is where you are. And because He's beside you, you cannot get lost. The guidance of Your good shepherd will meet you where you are. All you need to do is remember that comforting, calming truth.

*THANK YOU, LORD, FOR ALWAYS BEING
WITH ME EVERYWHERE I GO AND IN EVERY
SITUATION I ENCOUNTER. MAY I BECOME
EVER MINDFUL OF THAT TRUTH.*

EASE ON DOWN THE ROAD

DEMONSTRATE Your ways, O Eternal One. Teach me to understand so I can follow. EASE me down the path of Your truth. FEED me Your word because You are the True God who has saved me. I wait all day long, hoping, trusting in You.

PSALM 25:4–5 VOICE

Jesus is our example, the one who demonstrates the ways of God, the Son who "watches the Father closely and then mimics the work of the Father" (John 5:19 VOICE). He is also our teacher, His Word full of stories we can readily understand and from which we can learn how to truly live. Jesus' example, His teachings, His Word are what we are to nourish our inner warrior woman with. He is the one we learn to wait for, trust in, and hope in.

Jesus was a servant filled with compassion. He had the courage to speak the truth and the strength to take on people's burdens, and He taught His followers to treat others as they would like to be treated. Loving as He loved, giving as He gave, and living as He lived is a good place to start as we ease on down the way, our footsteps on the path He trod.

JESUS, I WANT TO BE LIKE YOU. TEACH ME
HOW TO HAVE COURAGE, COMPASSION,
AND CALM, LIVING AND LOVING AS YOU DID.
GIVE ME A SERVANT'S HEART AS I LIVE FOR YOU.

THE RELEASE AND RELIEF
OF FORGIVENESS

And forgive us our debts, as we also have forgiven (left, remitted,
and let go of the debts, and have given up resentment against)
our debtors. . . . For if you forgive people their trespasses [their
reckless and willful sins, leaving them, letting them go, and giving
up resentment], your heavenly Father will also forgive you.

MATTHEW 6:12, 14 AMPC

Jesus never held any grudges. Can you imagine what that feels like?

Consider what your life would be like if you allowed what other people said about you or did to you—whether intentional or unintentional—to roll off your shoulders and onto Jesus' shoulders. All the angst, stress, and bitterness of the unforgiveness you now carry would no longer be yours to bear. You'd no longer be weighed down with thoughts of vengeance, no longer burned out by flames of resentment.

Forgiving someone is more for you than for the one you are forgiving. After all, they have already gone along their merry way, not a care in the world. Yet you still may be holding on to the pain they've inflicted until it fades into a kind of lingering bitterness that continues to burn you like acid.

Jesus has forgiven you over and over again. Now it's time for you to forgive—and go along your merry way.

> HELP ME, LORD. GIVE ME THE DESIRE,
> THE WILL, AND THE STRENGTH TO FORGIVE
> ALL, JUST AS YOU'VE FORGIVEN ME.

BLOOMING—
NO MATTER WHAT!

But blessed is the one who trusts in Me alone;
the Eternal will be his confidence. He is like a tree planted
by water, sending out its roots beside the stream. It does
not fear the heat or even drought. Its leaves stay green
and its fruit is dependable, no matter what it faces.
JEREMIAH 17:7–8 VOICE

Speaking through the prophet Jeremiah, God tells us that the one who trusts in her own—and other mere mortals'—strengths and abilities are cursed! She is like a shrub in the desert that never grows. Nothing good will come her way. She'll forever live in an eternal wasteland, empty within and without.

Yet those who trust in God alone, who make Him their hope and confidence, will be like a tree planted beside a stream. *"No matter what it faces,"* it won't fear, and will continue to grow true and strong, and be forever fruitful!

Yes, it's true. You're only human. You may have those days when you find yourself trusting a fellow human you can see instead of God, an invisible omnipotent power. But don't go far down that path—because it's only by trusting God that the impossible becomes possible. Only with God can you stay green and continue to dream, to bloom wherever you're planted, no matter what.

HELP ME TRUST YOU AND YOU ALONE, LORD,
SO THAT I WILL CONTINUE TO BLOOM IN PEACE
AND PROSPERITY—NO MATTER WHAT!

ONLY ONE PLACE TO GO

Her husband Elkanah said, "Oh, Hannah, why are
you crying? Why aren't you eating? And why are you
so upset? Am I not of more worth to you than ten sons?"
So Hannah ate. Then she pulled herself together,
slipped away quietly, and entered the sanctuary.
1 SAMUEL 1:8–9 MSG

Hannah was one of the two wives of Elkanah. The other was Peninnah. She had children, but Hannah had none.

Every year when the families would travel down to Shiloh to worship and sacrifice to the Lord, Elkanah would serve a portion of the animal sacrificed to Peninnah and her children, then a double portion to Hannah, whom he loved more. This infuriated Peninnah, who grew to hate Hannah for her preferential treatment and would taunt her for her barrenness, reducing Hannah to tears.

We may have all the love in the world from one special person, and although that love itself is a blessing, it may not make up for the trials and tribulations we sometimes must bear. But there is someone we can seek—a person who is the very definition of love itself. In Him we will find the relief we're searching for.

When you are lower than low, there's only one place to go—to the feet of God. He's your biggest fan and encourager, the doer of miracles, the God with the plan.

HERE I AM, LORD, AT YOUR FEET. IT IS
YOU ALONE WHO I NEED AND SEEK.

TEARS IN A BOTTLE

It so happened that the priest Eli was sitting in a place of
honor beside the doorpost of the Eternal's congregation tent
as Hannah entered. She was heartbroken, and she began to
pray to the Eternal One, weeping uncontrollably as she did.

1 Samuel 1:9–10 voice

We've all had those times when we are so low, our heart so cracked, that we cannot keep our tears from gushing forth. That's where we find Hannah, "in distress of soul, praying to the Lord and weeping bitterly" (1 Samuel 1:10 ampc).

When you're heart-weary and soul-withered, when you can no longer see through the tears, turn to God. In the darkness of your room, He waits, watching with compassion and concern. His intense desire is for you to turn to Him so that He can hold you close, rock you, and love you.

Do not think yourself weak for the tears. It's a natural reaction to the heartbreaks that come our way. The tears cleanse and relieve us. So allow yourself to cry. But when the tears subside, resolve to seek the love and light of God and experience the balm of comfort and hope He provides.

WHEN I GO THROUGH DARK TIMES, LORD,
I PRAY THAT YOU, THE ONE WHO KEEPS TRACK
OF ALL MY SORROWS AND COLLECTS MY PRECIOUS
TEARS IN A BOTTLE [PSALM 56:8], WOULD
COMFORT ME WITH YOUR LIGHT AND LOVE.

KEEP PRAYING

Hannah was praying in her heart, silently. Her lips moved,
but no sound was heard. Eli jumped to the conclusion that
she was drunk. He approached her and said, "You're drunk!
How long do you plan to keep this up? Sober up, woman!"

1 SAMUEL 1:12–14 MSG

Poor Hannah. There she was, in intense sorrow, not speaking aloud but praying her heart out before the Lord. And the priest Eli accused her of being drunk!

When others' lives are going well and they pass you by in a lighthearted way or accuse you of gross misconduct, keep on praying. Keep on pouring out your heart to God. And continue on until your soul is emptied of all the sorrow and pain that has weighed it down. Keep praying, even if your request to God seems an impossibility. Keep praying, though your back gets weary and your knees sore. Keep praying until all that needs to be unburdened now rests with God instead of with you. Keep praying until, you, like Hannah, can rise full of hope and promise.

I COME BEFORE YOU, LORD, LETTING MY TEARS
FALL FREELY ON YOUR SHOULDER. YOU KNOW MY
PAIN AND MY PETITION. I PRAY THAT YOU WOULD
MEND MY BROKEN HEART AND FILL ME WITH THE
HOPE AND PROMISE I CAN FIND ONLY IN YOU.

REMEMBERED

*Afterward, they returned home to Ramah. Then Elkanah
was intimate with his wife Hannah, and the LORD
remembered her. After some time, Hannah conceived
and gave birth to a son. She named him Samuel,
because she said, "I requested him from the LORD."*

1 SAMUEL 1:19–20 HCSB

God knows you like a book. He doesn't just know all your sorrows, all your desires, all your prayers, and all your petitions. He also remembers you.

Perhaps you think God has forgotten all about you. Those petitions you sent up years ago are still unanswered. Your dreams have withered. Perhaps God has lost track of you.

No way. That's impossible. Why? Because God has made it clear that you are forever on His mind: "Can a mother forget the infant at her breast, walk away from the baby she bore? But even if mothers forget, I'd never forget you—never. Look, I've written your names on the backs of my hands" (Isaiah 49:15–16 MSG).

How wonderful to have a God who's on your side, whose vision of your face, form, mind, soul, and spirit are continually before Him. He has a grand plan for His people. And you are a part of that plan. You have been and always will be remembered.

*THANK YOU, LORD, FOR ALWAYS CARING ABOUT ME,
LOVING ME, LEADING ME, REMEMBERING ME. FOR
WRITING MY NAME ON THE BACK OF YOUR HANDS.*

STANDING APART

*As part of their assimilation into Babylonian court life,
the king offered them a daily portion of food and wine
from his own table. . . . Daniel was determined not to
violate God's law and defile himself by eating the food
and drinking the wine that came from the king's table.*

DANIEL 1:5, 8 VOICE

God allowed Nebuchadnezzar of Babylon to overtake Judah. This involved not only taking members of Judah's royal family and the nobility as prisoner, but robbing God's temple and carrying everything home to Babylon.

King Nebuchadnezzar's goal was to assimilate the best of the royals and nobles of Judah into Babylonian culture. Doing so would further cripple the defeated nation, for they wouldn't want to attack Babylon because some of their own lived there.

Daniel and his Judean friends had no desire to become part of this pagan nation. So they proposed that for ten days they'd eat only veggies and drink only water rather than eating the king's food. Their keeper agreed. After the ten-day trial, Daniel and his friends appeared healthier than those who ate the king's food and drank his wine.

This world will pull at us, try to assimilate us into its ways. But we, like Daniel and his friends, are not part of this foreign land (1 Chronicles 29:15). God will give us the courage to stand with Him apart from this world.

GIVE ME THE COURAGE, LORD, TO STAND SEPARATE
FROM THE WORLD BUT AS ONE WITH YOU.

IN POSITION

*God had given Daniel special favor and fondness in the eyes
of the king's chief eunuch. . . . The king interviewed all of
them and found that none of the candidates were any better
than Daniel, Hananiah, Mishael, and Azariah; so they were
each assigned an important place in the king's court.*

DANIEL 1:9, 19 VOICE

Imagine having your country overrun by another, then being taken
forcibly from home and plopped down in a foreign place. You're
to learn a new language and try to assimilate into a culture and
society very different from your own.

You may begin to wonder where God is, why He isn't looking
out for you in this situation. But the thing is, He's already there. In
fact, He planned this scenario. In it you are going to be favored.
And you are going to be in a position to do what He needs done.

That's how it went with Daniel. First, he gained favor with
his keeper; then the king found Daniel and his friends "ten times
better than all. . .who were in his whole realm" (Daniel 1:20 AMPC).
This would put all four of these God-fearing men in a position of
influence in this foreign land.

You too are favored by God. He has chosen you for His purposes.
You are now in a position to do what He needs done. Your only role
is to stay open to His will and way—and follow both.

HERE I AM, LORD. USE ME AS YOU WILL.

PRAYER POWER

Daniel went to his house and told his friends Hananiah,
Mishael, and Azariah about the matter, urging them to
ask the God of heaven for mercy concerning this mystery,
so Daniel and his friends would not be killed with the rest of
Babylon's wise men. The mystery was then revealed to Daniel
in a vision at night, and Daniel praised the God of heaven.

DANIEL 2:17–19 HCSB

Things were tense in Babylon. King Nebuchadnezzar had a strange dream, and none of the wise men and magicians in his court could explain its meaning. Not being able to make the matter clear to the king meant a death sentence for the king's wise men, which included Daniel and his friends.

So Daniel explained the situation to his friends and urged them to ask God to explain the mystery. And God answered their prayers. He blessed Daniel with a vision, revealing the enigma that no human could unravel.

Prayer is powerful—even more so when two or more pray together. Make prayer the first weapon in your arsenal.

LORD, THANK YOU FOR PROVIDING ME WITH
THE POWER OF PRAYER. MAY IT—AND YOU—
BE THE FIRST THING I TURN TO WHEN I NEED
HELP, STRENGTH, COURAGE, AND ANSWERS.

A CONDUIT OF LIGHT

He reveals deep truths and hidden secrets; He knows what lies
veiled in the darkness; pure light radiates from within Him.
I recognize who You are, and I praise You, God of my ancestors,
for You have given me wisdom and strength. And now You
have graciously revealed to me what we asked of You.

DANIEL 2:22–23 VOICE

Having received an answer to the prayers of himself and his friends, Daniel gave credit and praise to God. And in his praise, Daniel made it clear that he recognized who God is and that God is the one who had given him all the wisdom and strength he needed in this foreign land.

Then, when Daniel went before the king to tell him what his dream meant, he told him, "I am here today, not because I have greater wisdom than any other in the land, but because God in His wisdom has revealed this mystery to me. It is God's plan that the king knows the meaning of this dream and understands the thoughts that raced through your mind" (Daniel 2:30 VOICE). In giving God the credit, Daniel's humility made room for King Nebuchadnezzar to catch a glimpse of the Eternal One and to praise Him himself (Daniel 2:47).

You, warrior woman, are a conduit through which others may see God. Allow His light and wisdom to shine through you and directly upon others.

LORD, MAY I BE THE CONDUIT THROUGH
WHICH OTHERS FEEL AND SEE YOUR LIGHT.

ALIVE WITH FAITH

If you throw us into the blazing furnace, then the God we serve
is able to rescue us from a furnace of blazing fire and release
us from your power, Your Majesty. But even if He does not,
O king, you can be sure that we still will not serve your gods
and we will not worship the golden statue you erected.

DANIEL 3:17–18 VOICE

"People alive with faith" (Hebrews 11:33 VOICE)—that's what Shadrach, Meshach, and Abednego were.

King Nebuchadnezzar had a golden statue made "90 feet high and 9 feet wide" (Daniel 3:1 VOICE). People of all nations were commanded to bow down and worship it whenever they heard music play. If they did not follow this edict from the king, they'd be thrown into a fiery furnace—which meant certain death.

Shadrach, Meshach, and Abednego defied the king's order. When questioned by Nebuchadnezzar, they made their position clear. The only God they'd bow down to was their own. And if Nebuchadnezzar decided to throw them into a furnace because of their refusal, so be it. God would rescue them—or not. No matter the consequences, they'd continue to follow the Lord, not the king.

Ask God to help your inner warrior woman be steadfast in faith, trusting Him regardless of the circumstances or possible outcomes.

BLESS ME, LORD, WITH THE COOL AND
CALM OF TRUE DEVOTION TO YOU.

THE DIVINE COMPANION

*"Look!" Nebuchadnezzar shouted. "I see four men, unbound,
walking around in the fire unharmed! And the fourth looks like
a god!" . . . Then the high officers, officials, governors, and
advisers crowded around them and saw that the fire had not
touched them. Not a hair on their heads was singed, and their
clothing was not scorched. They didn't even smell of smoke!*

DANIEL 3:25, 27 NLT

God will meet you in the fires of this life. He will be with you through
every situation, never allowing you to walk alone.

It's when the flames begin to lick at your heels that you'll start
to realize that His holy presence resides within you, around you,
before you, and behind you. There you understand that you really
have nothing to fear. And there, amid the flames, He will loosen the
ties that bind you. Meanwhile, the rest of your being will remain
untouched, unhurt, unscorched. Not a hair on your head will perish.

When you walk alongside your divine companion, when you
put all your hopes, dreams, and trust in Him, you, warrior woman,
will become a hero of faith.

> THANK YOU, JESUS, FOR WALKING BESIDE
> ME, LOVING ME, CARING FOR ME, MAKING
> ME A PART OF YOUR LIGHT AND LIFE.

COMPASSION FOR ALL

Aram, on one of its raiding expeditions against Israel,
captured a young girl who became a maid to Naaman's
wife. One day she said to her mistress, "Oh, if only
my master could meet the prophet of Samaria,
he would be healed of his skin disease."

2 KINGS 5:1–2 MSG

A young girl had been taken away from her home and out of her country of Israel by foreigners. Now, she served as a maid to the wife of Naaman, a "commander of the army of the king of Syria. . .also a mighty man of valor, but he was a leper" (2 Kings 5:1 AMPC).

This young servant girl could also be called a mighty person of valor. What made her brave, compassionate, and a blessing was her faith. She could have been bitter about her fate. She could have kept the idea of a cure away from the ears of her mistress and master, as a sort of revenge against their people: *If only they knew. . .but I won't be the one to tell them. After what they did to me. . .*

Resentment, bitterness, and vengefulness can stifle not only our faith but our compassion for others—whether they are worthy of it or not. A warrior woman with compassion and a desire to bless others is a prize to any household, any job, any region, any country.

LORD, FILL ME WITH A HEART OF COMPASSION
FOR ALL. MAKE ME A BLESSING.

SWEET SLEEP

You, Eternal One, wrap around me like an impenetrable shield. . . . I lift my voice to You, Eternal One, and You answer me from Your sacred heights. . . . I lie down at night and fall asleep. I awake in the morning—healthy, strong, vibrant—because the Eternal supports me.

PSALM 3:3–5 VOICE

Women are more prone to sleeping problems than men. That's because we have a lot more going on in our bodies. The change in our hormones during our menstrual cycle, pregnancy, and menopause can affect our ability to get a good night's sleep. And without true rest at night, we can have a difficult time being a warrior woman for God.

So what's a woman to do? Turn to God's Word before she turns out the light.

Today's verses remind us of who God is in essence and to us. He is eternal. He will be there throughout and beyond our lives. He is our impenetrable shield, wrapped around us like our favorite blanket. In Him we have all the safety and security we need.

Problems? Pray about them before you shut your eyes, knowing that God is bending His ear down to your lips, taking in every word, sentence, pause, and sigh. Imagine yourself resting in His hand that He holds close to His chest. Fall asleep to the rhythm of your breath, your heartbeat, aligned with His.

AH, LORD. HOLD ME CLOSE. HEAR MY WHISPERED PRAYER. BE MY SHIELD AND COMFORT. I REST IN YOU.

ANGELS ON THE WAY

As Jacob started on his way again,
angels of God came to meet him.
GENESIS 32:1 NLT

Jacob was about to face his brother, Esau. The one he'd cheated out of a birthright and their father Isaac's blessing. Jacob had no army with him. Just his livestock, servants, wives, and children. He may have felt defenseless. But as he started on his way, he was met by God's angels.

God's Word tells us that "the messenger of the Eternal God surrounds everyone who walks with Him and is always there to protect and rescue us" (Psalm 34:7 VOICE). That God "will order his angels to protect you wherever you go" (Psalm 91:11 NLT) when you, like Jacob, are "greatly afraid and distressed" (Genesis 32:7 AMPC).

Are your eyes open to the angels around you, the ones who come in response to your prayers and pleas? "Isn't it obvious that all angels are sent to help out with those lined up to receive salvation?" (Hebrews 1:14 MSG).

Keep your eyes, mind, heart, and spirit open to the angels, their presence, their help. As you go on your way, know that they will be there to meet you, help you, protect you, and guide you.

WHEN I AM AFRAID AND DISTRESSED, LORD,
SEND YOUR ANGELS TO MEET ME AS I GO ON MY WAY.
OPEN MY EYES TO THEIR PRESENCE. MAY THEY BLESS
ME WITH STRENGTH, CALM, AND CONFIDENCE.

UNTROUBLED HEARTS

Do not let your hearts be troubled (distressed, agitated).
You believe in and adhere to and trust in and rely on
God; believe in and adhere to and trust in and rely also
on Me. In My Father's house there are many dwelling
places (homes). If it were not so, I would have told you;
for I am going away to prepare a place for you.
JOHN 14:1–2 AMPC

Jesus implores you not to be troubled in this world, not to get lost in the darkness of despair. Instead, believe in God. Trust in Him. Stick to Him like glue. Rely on Him in every aspect of your life. And do the same with Jesus.

God's Son, the one called the Sun of Righteousness, who comes with healing in His wings (Malachi 4:2 AMPC), wants you to trust Him for everything—strength, confidence, calm, courage, love, compassion, and so much more. He wants you to know that He is always here, forever by your side. Yet He has also gone ahead of you to prepare a place for you, to make arrangements for you, to greet you when you arrive at His Father's house.

Envision Jesus sitting beside you, saying, "Don't let your heart be troubled. I am here for you and always will be so that you can be where I am." Then rest in that peace He provides.

THANK YOU, LORD, FOR BEING IN MY
LIFE AND FOR PREPARING A HOME FOR
ME WHERE I MAY LIVE WITH YOU FOREVER.

CALL THE COMFORTER

I will ask the Father, and He will give you another Comforter
(Counselor, Helper, Intercessor, Advocate, Strengthener,
and Standby), that He may remain with you forever—
the Spirit of Truth. . . . You know and recognize Him,
for He lives with you [constantly] and will be in you.
JOHN 14:16–17 AMPC

Imagine that. Within you is a Comforter, the Holy Spirit. He will advise you, help you, intercede for you, and strengthen you. He is always on standby, ever prepared to hear your prayers. He will even interpret the groans and moans that erupt from the very center of your being.

When courage abandons you, fear grips you, and you feel as if you can't walk another step, take on another challenge, or even lift your head off your pillow, call on the Comforter. Allow the Holy Spirit to meld with your spirit. Know that He is close and will relay your messages, your moans, your groans, your tears, and your heartaches to the Father and Son, who will move mountains to help you wherever you are.

This Comforter, the Holy Spirit, is within you to remind you of all that Jesus has said, to provide you with the strength and courage and calm you need no matter what the circumstances or time of day. Call. He will respond.

MY DEAR COMFORTER, HEAR MY PRAYER,
MY PLEA. GIVE ME THE PEACE, STRENGTH,
AND CONFIDENCE I SO DESPERATELY NEED.

TUNE IN

A sound mind makes for a robust body, but runaway emotions corrode the bones. . . . A cheerful disposition is good for your health; gloom and doom leave you bone-tired.

PROVERBS 14:30, 17:22 MSG

It's commendable to want to keep up with current events, read the newspaper, listen to podcasts, and watch the news. Yet the news that is usually relayed to the public is often the bad news. Really bad news.

Crazy weather, warring nations, starving children, domestic abuse, shootings, not to mention nonstop political wrangling—it's enough to make you want to crawl into bed and pull the covers over your head.

Yet God would have you be a light in this dark world—a woman who, filled with His Spirit, is a comfort and balm to those she comes in contact with, a woman who is courageous and strong no matter what the latest headline.

To keep up your energy and courage, do yourself and the world a favor and spend more time tuned into God's Word than man's. Doing so will promote a calm and undisturbed mind as well as a happy heart. You'll begin to see things from God's perspective of peace and strength rather than mayhem and helplessness. Just what a warrior woman needs to get her through not just the day but her entire life.

LORD, REMIND ME TO ATTEND MORE TO YOUR GOOD NEWS THAN THE NEWS OF THIS WORLD.

SING YOUR DESIRE

*[So I went with him, and when we were climbing the
rocky steps up the hillside, my beloved shepherd said to
me] O my dove, [while you are here] in the seclusion of the
clefts in the solid rock, in the sheltered and secret place
of the cliff, let me see your face, let me hear your voice;
for your voice is sweet, and your face is lovely. [My heart
was touched and I fervently sang to him my desire].*

SONG OF SOLOMON 2:14–15 AMPC

Every warrior woman has a soft side. Jesus makes His appeal to
her, encouraging her to come with Him, to walk by His side. And
then, as the good shepherd, He speaks to her with love and adoration in His eyes.

Jesus calls you His dove and asks that you, while you are
secluded with Him, sheltered in that secret place, show Him your
beautiful face—the one with which God has blessed you. Jesus
wants you to lift your sweet voice, to whisper into His ear, to tell
Him all that's on your heart.

From your heart, sing your praises to Him. Let Him know the
gratitude that swells your soul—all the little things He has done
with you and for you. Tell Him your innermost desire, the thing for
which you need His help the most.

Lift your voice to your beloved, singing your desire.

BELOVED SHEPHERD, I YEARN FOR. . .

GOD IS HERE

"The God of my father has been with me." . . . "And be
sure of this: I am with you always, even to the end of
the age." . . . The Lᴏʀᴅ is my light and my salvation—
so why should I be afraid? The Lᴏʀᴅ is my fortress,
protecting me from danger, so why should I tremble?

Genesis 31:5; Matthew 28:20; Psalm 27:1 nlt

There's one thing the warrior woman must have clear in her mind. And that is that her Father, His Son Jesus, and the Holy Spirit are always with her—*always.*

God repeats this truth over and over again in His Word. And Jesus reiterates it, telling His followers that He will be with them always. *You* sitting right there, reading this right now. You are not alone. Ever. God is always by your side.

And because God is by your side—constantly and consistently—you never need to be afraid. He is the one who brings the light when you find yourself groping around in the darkness. He is the one who will save you when no one or nothing else can. He is the one who brings an army of angels with Him when needed. He will surround you with an impenetrable shield when the volley of insults, hurts, and angers begin to flow.

Never fear. God is here!

MY FEAR IS GONE, BECAUSE I KNOW YOU'RE HERE, GOD!

TAPPING INTO PEACE

Peace I leave with you; My [own] peace I now give
and bequeath to you. Not as the world gives do I give to
you. Do not let your hearts be troubled, neither let them
be afraid. [Stop allowing yourselves to be agitated and
disturbed; and do not permit yourselves to be fearful
and intimidated and cowardly and unsettled.]

JOHN 14:27 AMPC

Need peace? You have it when you tap into the presence of Jesus.

The world is filled with turmoil. But Jesus tells you not to let such outside forces disturb your inner woman. The Amplified Bible adds some explanatory text that helps you get a handle on this truth, clearly telling you in no uncertain terms to "stop allowing yourselves to be agitated and disturbed; and do not permit yourselves to be fearful and intimidated and cowardly and unsettled." By keeping these words in mind, when you feel fear beginning to creep into your heart and mind, stop! Don't allow it to take hold. Remember who you are—a daughter of the King, a sister of the Prince of Peace, a keeper of a Comforter and Counselor.

You, warrior woman, have all you need to keep that peace of Jesus, to tap into its power and remain calm, cool, confident, and collected every moment of your life.

I PRAISE AND THANK YOU, LORD, FOR YOUR PRESENCE
IN MY LIFE! WITH YOU NEAR, I HAVE NO FEAR!

MORE THAN ENOUGH

"God has been very gracious to me.
I have more than enough."
GENESIS 33:11 NLT

These are the words Jacob said to Esau, insisting that his brother accept the gift he'd brought him, hoping to appease the man he'd tricked.

These are also words that, by themselves, can soothe your soul, because they remind you that it is your God who has given you all you could ever need—and more!

In a society where people continually crave the next new thing and perpetually pine for more and more, today's verse tells you that you really don't need more. What you already have is more than adequate to keep you.

So, when you desire that new dress when you already have a full closet, or you feel you can't live without the latest bestseller, stop for a moment. Consider the fact that you already have more than enough because God has been so gracious to you. Then, instead of getting something more, consider what you have that you might give away to someone who needs it. Perhaps a nice outfit that you rarely wear. Or a book or two that you could donate. Then maybe take a trip to the library and put yourself on the list to borrow that latest bestseller you've been wanting to read.

Calm the "I want" yearnings within you, confident that you really already have more than enough.

LORD, THANK YOU FOR ALL YOUR BLESSINGS,
FOR GIVING ME MORE THAN I COULD EVER NEED.

JUST UNRATTLED

Nothing will ever rattle them; the just will always be remembered.
They will not be afraid when the news is bad because they have
resolved to trust in the Eternal. Their hearts are confident, and
they are fearless, for they expect to see their enemies defeated.

PSALM 112:6–8 VOICE

When you live a life right with God and trust in Him for *everything*,
nothing can rattle you! Your inner warrior woman will be fearless!

The Bible repeats this truth over and over again: if we
will just trust in God, taking His Word to heart, we will not
be afraid—no matter how bad the news! Yet, along with
this trust and right living, we are to live with a sense of expectation.
We are to have that hope within us that God will be true to His
word. That He will hear our prayers and answer them. That we are
destined to receive nothing but good from His hands.

This doesn't mean we'll understand all that happens to us and
those we love. But it does mean that we have an understanding
God, one who knows what it means to be betrayed, disbelieved,
mocked, and insulted. One who knows just what we need to rise
above all that the world gives us and take what heaven offers.

ALL PRAISE TO YOU, LORD, FOR GIVING ME CONFIDENCE
AND COURAGE IN ALL WAYS EVERY DAY.

THE LEARNING CURVE

*The Eternal is the source of my strength and the shield that
guards me. When I learn to rest and truly trust Him, He
sends His help. This is why my heart is singing! I open my
mouth to praise Him, and thankfulness rises as song.*

PSALM 28:7 VOICE

When it comes to faith, there is a learning curve. But if we are dili-
gent in seeking the Lord through His Word, the pathway to courage
and calm will become clearer and clearer with each passing day.

Psalm 28:7 reminds us that the strength we seek is in God. By
realizing that His presence surrounds each one of us, we will feel
as if *in Him*, we can do anything and everything, even the things
our human minds label "impossible."

Today, seek that pathway. Learn to rest in and truly trust God
for all you need and in all you do. Know that He is there whenever
and wherever you need Him. As you do so, you will find all the
cares of this world falling away. Free of what can hinder you, you
will be unable to keep from singing His praises, thanking Him for
being in your life, for shining His light into your darkness.

LORD, YOU ARE MY STRENGTH AND SONG, MY SHIELD
AND PEACE. TEACH ME HOW TO TRUST IN YOU,
TO REALIZE AND SEEK OUT YOUR MAGNIFICENT
AND CALMING PRESENCE EVERY DAY.

LED BY THE SPIRIT, MET BY ANGELS

Immediately the [Holy] Spirit [from within] drove Him out into the wilderness (desert), and He stayed in the wilderness (desert) forty days, being tempted [all the while] by Satan; and He was with the wild beasts, and the angels ministered to Him [continually].

MARK 1:12–13 AMPC

After Jesus' baptism in the Jordan, the Holy Spirit led Him into a challenge. The wilderness. A desert. An arid and unfriendly place. Jesus was among wild beasts, surrounded by danger. Yet, even there, the angels ministered to Him.

You too will have challenges to face. You may at times find yourself in an inhospitable place, whether that be physically, emotionally, mentally, financially, or spiritually. Danger may surround you. Yet, even there, God will meet you. He will send His Spirit to guide and guard you. He will encompass you with His angels who will minister to your every need.

Because you are God's daughter, one of His precious children, you don't ever need to fear. Just look for the Father, His Spirit, His Son, and His angels, who are forever near, waiting and wanting to help.

HOW COMFORTING, LORD, TO KNOW THAT YOU ARE CONSTANTLY WITH ME, SENDING AID TO HELP ME GET THROUGH THE WILDERNESS AND DANGERS OF THIS LIFE. LEAD ME TO THE PLACE YOU WOULD HAVE ME LEARN AND GROW.

HOW TO SUCCEED

They fought against the Hagrites, Jetur, Naphish, and Nodab.
God helped them as they fought. God handed the Hagrites and
all their allies over to them, because they cried out to him during
the battle. God answered their prayers because they trusted
him. . . . Many were killed, because the battle was God's.

1 CHRONICLES 5:19–20, 22 MSG

God will help us in the skirmishes of life—*if* we will cry out to Him for help. He will answer our prayers—*if* we will trust Him. And our victory will be assured—*if* we're engaged in His battle.

Walking the way of God is not a one- but a two-way street. We cannot just assume that God will help us. We have to *ask* Him for help—folding our hands and praying under our breath or shouting at the top of our lungs! He will answer our pleas if we rely on Him, cling to Him, trust in *Him*, and not in our own strength, skill, and courage. And if the battle is God's, if it is one that He put in our path and directed, assisted, and led us into, we will emerge victorious.

Pray to God. Trust Him for all. Answer the call. And you will succeed.

THANK YOU, LORD, FOR TEACHING ME HOW TO BE
YOUR WARRIOR WOMAN, TO PRAY, TRUST, AND LET YOU
LEAD. THEN I KNOW I WILL SUCCEED—IN YOU.

GOD'S SPIRIT AND POWER

I was unsure of how to go about this, and felt totally inadequate—I was scared to death, if you want the truth of it—and so nothing I said could have impressed you or anyone else. But the Message came through anyway. God's Spirit and God's power did it.

1 CORINTHIANS 2:3–4 MSG

Ever been there? You find yourself unsure about how to do something that God has prompted you to do. You feel inadequate, wondering why God chose you for this particular task. You are certain that nothing you could say would inspire anyone. Yet the deed is done, the speech is made anyway. How? Not through your own power, certainly, but through the power of the Holy Spirit working through you.

This takes the pressure off in regard to anything God moves you to do. All you are is the vehicle, the tool He uses for His purposes. That makes "it clear that your life of faith is a response to God's power, not to some fancy mental or emotional footwork" (1 Corinthians 2:5 MSG).

Once your inner warrior woman understands that it's God's power and Spirit that do the work that needs to be done, all worries and fears melt away. All she needs to do is tap into God and let Him take the lead.

HELP ME, LORD, TO SET MYSELF ASIDE AND LET YOUR SPIRIT AND POWER SHINE THROUGH!

KEEPING THE FAITH

*During Peter's imprisonment, the church prayed constantly
and intensely to God for his safety. Their prayers were not
answered, until the night before Peter's execution.*

ACTS 12:5–6 VOICE

King Herod had already ordered the apostle James to be killed by
the sword. Realizing how much this pleased the Jews, he went even
further, arresting Peter and throwing him in jail. The king assigned
four squads of soldiers (sixteen armed men) to guard him. After
Passover, Herod planned to bring Peter to trial.

The church was praying—not only continually but intensely—
for Peter, hoping God would save their friend and fellow Christ
follower. Day after day was slipping away, and still Peter remained
in prison. Yet, at the very last minute—"the night before Peter's
execution"—God intervened in a very dramatic way.

There are times when there is no other way for us but through
prayer. Yet with that prayer we must be patient, remembering that
all is done in God's timing, not ours. And we must not give up but
persist in our fervent and constant prayers, knowing that if it is
God's will, it will be done. We must simply keep the faith.

> HELP ME, LORD, TO REMEMBER THAT ALL IS
> DONE IN YOUR TIMING, NOT MINE. HELP ME
> PRAY CONSISTENTLY, NEVER GIVING UP,
> AND LEAVE THE RESULTS IN YOUR HANDS.

IN GOD'S HANDS

Then the time came for Herod to bring him out for the kill.
That night, even though shackled to two soldiers, one on either
side, Peter slept like a baby. And there were guards at the door
keeping their eyes on the place. Herod was taking no chances!

ACTS 12:6 MSG

Talk about faith! Peter was chained to two soldiers. He knew they were planning to kill him the next day. And there he was, in his cell, sleeping like a baby!

What would it be like to have that kind of faith—a faith that helps you to realize that whatever happens, all will be well? Either way, dead or alive, you are in God's hands—which is truly the best and only place to be!

Humans can make plans and do their worst to us. But it doesn't really matter what they plan or actually do. Nothing they might bring against us can touch the warrior woman within. Why? Because God is with us and has promised never to leave us. He has our names written on His hands.

Think on this today. Remind yourself that no matter what happens, God is always with you—and with Him is the only place to be. So sleep soundly. God's got you!

THANK YOU, LORD, FOR KEEPING ME IN YOUR HANDS,
THE SAFEST PLACE TO BE ON HEAVEN OR EARTH.

TOUCHED BY GOD

Suddenly, there was a bright light in the cell, and an angel of the Lord stood before Peter. The angel struck him on the side to awaken him and said, "Quick! Get up!" And the chains fell off his wrists. Then the angel told him, "Get dressed and put on your sandals." And he did. "Now put on your coat and follow me."

ACTS 12:7–8 NLT

God's people prayed, and He responded in a big way.

Peter was sleeping soundly between two guards. Suddenly a bright light filled his cell. But that didn't waken the faith-filled Peter. So the angel had to nudge him to rouse him from his sleep.

The Lord's angel told a still somewhat groggy Peter to get up and be quick about it. The chains that had once held the prisoner simply fell off, allowing Peter to rise without waking the two guards beside him! The angel then ordered Peter to dress, put on shoes and his coat, and follow him out the door. Peter did so trustingly, not considering any obstacles before him.

God is in the details, touching upon every aspect of human life—from the threat of death to getting dressed, to following Him wherever He leads. Trust Him for everything.

THANK YOU, LORD, FOR DELIVERING ME, TOUCHING ME, CARING FOR ME, AND CALLING ME TO FOLLOW. IN YOU ALONE I TRUST. FOR YOU ALONE I WAIT. TO YOU ALONE I LISTEN.

DAZED AND DELIVERED

At the first intersection the angel left him, going his own way. That's when Peter realized it was no dream. "I can't believe it—this really happened! The Master sent his angel and rescued me from Herod's vicious little production and the spectacle the Jewish mob was looking forward to."

ACTS 12:10–11 MSG

God sometimes guides us while we are still dazed. In that condition, we are more pliable, more obedient to what He says. We're in no position to second-guess or analyze what is happening until it's all over. And it's only then, once we "come to ourselves," that we realize what God has done for us.

God is constantly delivering us, just as Jesus did from our sins. He gives us the freedom we need to live for Him. And then, oh what a wonderful change happens within us.

The next time you hear God's call, go—even if you aren't really sure what's happening. Trust Him for everything, placing yourself in His hands and allowing Him to lead you to safety away from your chains and into a place of freedom. Then, after the angel of God in your life goes his own way, only then will you be sure he was there at all.

IN YOUR HANDS I PLACE MYSELF, LORD. LEAD ME. I AM YOUR WILLING FOLLOWER.

REST EASY

He who dwells in the secret place of the Most High shall remain stable and fixed under the shadow of the Almighty [Whose power no foe can withstand]. I will say of the Lord, He is my Refuge and my Fortress, my God; on Him I lean and rely, and in Him I [confidently] trust!

PSALM 91:1–2 AMPC

Imagine that. When you live under the protection of God, when you abide in His presence, you are safe. Why? Because you are shielded by the Almighty—the one whose power no other force can withstand. God alone is your refuge and fortress from danger, panic, and fear—in heaven and on earth. And so the psalmist reminds you to say to yourself, "The Lord is my place of safety. On Him alone I will trust and rely. On Him alone I will lean."

When you have that kind of mindset, when you determine to seek out God and live under His protection, you will be rescued from every deadly trap. No matter what danger or difficulty comes your way, you can run to Him and find a haven in which you can rest and recover, knowing you are in the safest place you can be.

Find that comfort today. And rest easy.

I'M COMING TO YOU, LORD. FOR YOU ALONE ARE MY PLACE OF SAFETY, A HAVEN WHERE I CAN FIND COMFORT, CALM, AND CONFIDENCE NO MATTER WHAT MAY COME AGAINST ME.

UNDER HIS WINGS

Like a bird protecting its young, God will cover you with His feathers, will protect you under His great wings; His faithfulness will form a shield around you, a rock-solid wall to protect you.

PSALM 91:4 VOICE

Having trouble finding that place of God's presence? Close your eyes and imagine God as a huge mama bird, one who covers you with her feathers, pulling you close, so close that you can feel and hear her heart beating. In that place, in that cool shadow beneath her wings, you are protected from anyone and anything that might pose a danger to you, a threat to your life.

As you rest in that place of peace and safety, know that God will never leave you. He will never abandon you. His love and faithfulness toward you are like a shield that no one and nothing can ever penetrate. And it remains there for as long as you need it.

When you come to realize that there is no better shelter on earth or under heaven than God, all the worries and fears that have plagued you dissipate. Ah, what relief. What ease. What peace. What a refuge, nestled in God.

LORD, THANK YOU FOR LOVING ME SO MUCH, FOR PROVIDING FOR ME A PLACE OF PEACE WHERE I CAN NESTLE AGAINST YOU. YOU EASE MY HEART AND MIND. YOU ALLOW MY HEART AND SOUL TO FIND THE LOVE AND PROTECTION I HAVE SEARCHED FOR.

ANGELS WATCHING OVER YOU

*Because you have made the Lord your refuge, and the Most
High your dwelling place, there shall no evil befall you, nor any
plague or calamity come near your tent. For He will give His
angels [especial] charge over you to accompany and defend
and preserve you in all your ways [of obedience and service].*
PSALM 91:9–11 AMPC

Yes! It's true! God has given angels charge over you. They are
beside you. They walk with you. They will nudge you down the
right roads so that you do not lose your way. They will defend you
from whatever might come against you. They will be your guide
and guard you as you go along God's way.

Your guardian angels will also "bear you up on their hands, lest
you dash your foot against a stone" (Psalm 91:12 AMPC), keeping
you from stumbling. Keep these truths in mind when you walk
along God's highway, sticking to the path He has set before you.

Angels cared for and ministered to Jesus in the wilderness
when He was being tempted by the devil (Matthew 4:11). Another
angel came from heaven to strengthen Him when He was praying
in the garden of Gethsemane (Luke 22:43). As the angels helped
Jesus, they will help you. If you believe. . . If you trust. . .

*I DO BELIEVE, LORD, THAT YOU SEND ANGELS TO GUARD
AND GUIDE ME. MAY THEY MEET ME ON MY WAY!*

LOVE AND KNOW

Because he has set his love upon Me, therefore will
I deliver him; I will set him on high, because he knows
and understands My name [has a personal knowledge
of My mercy, love, and kindness—trusts and relies on
Me, knowing I will never forsake him, no, never].

PSALM 91:14 AMPC

All that God requires in return for His presence, protection, and guardian angels is for you to have an intimate, loving relationship with Him. That means seeking Him out, praising His name, reaching out, and placing yourself in His presence.

God wants you to know more about Him. To seek out His names and attributes in His Word. To trust that which He has done for others, He will do for you. To become familiar with His names—almighty God, the one who provides, good shepherd, God your rock, the one who heals, the one who hears, and so on—so that you will understand all He is to you.

God wants you to know that He will not only never leave you but will answer you whenever you call. He will respond, be by your side when there's trouble, and deliver you.

Love and know God, and you will experience heaven on earth.

I LOVE YOU, LORD. AND I WANT TO KNOW YOU
BETTER. TAKE ME THROUGH YOUR WORD. REVEAL
YOURSELF TO ME AS I TAKE MY REFUGE IN YOU.

ALL WELL

*Shunammite Woman (to her husband): I beg you to send
me a servant and a donkey so that I can go find Elisha,
the man of God. As soon as I do, I will come back here.*

*Father: Why is it that you are so anxious to find him today?
Today is not a holy day—a new moon or a Sabbath.*

Shunammite Woman: Don't worry; all will be well.

2 KINGS 4:22–23 VOICE

The childless Shunammite woman and her husband had built a little room for Elisha, the prophet who continually passed their house. Wanting to do something for her in return for her kindness, Elisha predicted she would bear a son in the next year. And, although thinking such a thing impossible, she did indeed have a baby boy!

Yet some years later, the boy died in her arms. She laid his body on Elisha's bed, closed the door, and told her husband she wanted to go and seek the prophet. But instead of telling him why, she simply reassured him, "Don't worry; all will be well." She was certain God would find a way where there seemed to be no way.

When we have confidence that God is the doer of the impossible, we too can tell ourselves and others, "Don't worry; all will be well."

**LORD, AS I LIVE AND BREATHE IN YOU, I LIVE WITH THE
CERTAINTY THAT ALL IS AND ALWAYS WILL BE WELL.**

PRAYER HABIT

When Daniel learned that the decree had been signed and posted,
he continued to pray just as he had always done. . . . Three times
a day he knelt there in prayer, thanking and praising his God.
DANIEL 6:10 MSG

Daniel had such great abilities, spirit, and intelligence that King Darius was planning to place him in charge of his entire kingdom. This didn't sit well with the other Persian administrators and high officials, so they came up with a way to get rid of Daniel.

Discovering that Daniel prayed three times a day to his God, they got the king to sign a decree saying that no one was to pray to any god or mortal other than King Darius. Anyone disobeying this edict would be thrown into the lions' den.

Daniel, *knowing that the decree had been signed,* "continued to pray just as he had always done." Nothing in heaven or on earth would keep Daniel from his daily time with the Lord.

There's nothing we can do without God's help. Empty vessels in His hands, we must ask daily for God's power, courage, and confidence, as well as His protection, guidance, and direction, ensuring that our path is aligned with His. A warrior woman will gain much strength and courage from the habit and power of persistent prayer!

HELP ME, LORD, TO BECOME AND REMAIN PERSISTENT
IN MY DAILY SPIRITUAL EXERCISES — MY PRAYERS,
PETITIONS, PRAISES, AND THANKS TO YOU!

NOT A SCRATCH!

"O king, live forever!" said Daniel. "My God sent his angel,
who closed the mouths of the lions so that they would not
hurt me. I've been found innocent before God and also
before you, O king. I've done nothing to harm you."

DANIEL 6:21–22 MSG

Daniel had prayed as he always had—three times a day with his windows opened toward Jerusalem. The reluctant Darius had no choice but to order him to be sent to the lions' den, yet he did try to encourage Daniel, telling him, "Your God, to whom you are so loyal, is going to get you out of this" (Daniel 6:16 MSG).

After enduring a sleepless night, the king ran to the lions' den the next day and called out, "Daniel, servant of the living God, has your God, whom you serve so loyally, saved you from the lions?" (Daniel 6:20 MSG).

He had! "When he was hauled up, there wasn't a scratch on him. He had trusted his God" (Daniel 6:23 MSG).

Warrior woman, be loyal to God. Entrust yourself to Him, resolving to remain confident in Him. And He will return that loyalty, trust, and confidence, leaving you without a scratch!

I ENTRUST MYSELF TO YOU, LORD. IN YOU
I AM CONFIDENT, ALLOWING NOTHING TO
COME BETWEEN ME AND THEE, KNOWING
YOU WILL ALWAYS REMAIN LOYAL TO ME!

BEFORE THE "AMEN"

"He stood before me and said, 'Daniel, I have come to make things plain to you. You had no sooner started your prayer when the answer was given. And now I'm here to deliver the answer to you. You are much loved! So listen carefully to the answer.' "

DANIEL 9:22–23 MSG

Daniel had been meditating on God's Word, then began to pray, asking God to have mercy for Jerusalem and His rebellious people. He continued to pray on and on, asking God for relief.

In response, Gabriel came to Daniel. The angel explained that no sooner had Daniel begun praying that an answer to his prayer had been given. And Gabriel was here to deliver that answer, to give Daniel insight and understanding about what God was going to do and why.

God sees and hears you pouring out your heart, crying your tears, understanding that you, a warrior woman, may have lost your courage and confidence or may have become weak and disheartened. Yet before you have even finished praying, His answer is on its way—perhaps being delivered by an angel who will give you the wisdom to understand it.

Take confidence, woman, that no matter what your state of heart, mind, soul, or spirit, God does hear your prayers. And He will respond before you say, "Amen"!

THANK YOU, LORD, FOR LOVING ME, HEARING ME, AND ANSWERING ME. . .BEFORE THE "AMEN"!

RELAX

"Relax. Don't be afraid," the household manager
told them. "Your God, the God of your father,
must have put this treasure into your sacks."

GENESIS 43:23 NLT

Joseph's brothers had paid for the grain they'd been given in Egypt. But on the way home, they discovered their money on top of their sacks.

So, on the second trip to Egypt, Joseph's brothers explained to the steward of Joseph's house what had happened. He immediately put their mind at ease by telling them to relax, not to worry about it or be afraid, because it was God who must have returned their money.

God is constantly watching over us, blessing us in ways we may not understand or perhaps even be aware of until some time has passed. Thus, we too might take these words—*Relax. Don't be afraid*—to heart or, rather, to mind.

"Relax. Don't be afraid" is a good mantra to memorize. In those moments of confusion, when we don't fully understand what's happening or why, we can remind our heart to rest easy, to keep in mind that we really have no reason to fear. God is always with us, looking out for us, blessing us step-by-step, day by day, in many amazing ways.

LORD, HELP ME WRITE, "RELAX. DON'T BE AFRAID," UPON MY MIND SO THAT WHEN FEAR BEGINS TO CREEP INTO MY HEART, I CAN REMEMBER THAT IN YOUR PROVIDENCE I AM CONTINUALLY CARED FOR AND BLESSED.

IN GOD ALONE

*Let the whole earth tremble before the LORD; let all
the inhabitants of the world stand in awe of Him. . . .
A king is not saved by a large army; a warrior will not
be delivered by great strength. The horse is a false hope
for safety; it provides no escape by its great power.*
PSALM 33:8, 16–17 HCSB

We trust so many things. That our bank account will never be depleted. That our car has ten more years. That our honeymoon will never end. That our body will always be youthful. That our job will keep us afloat financially. That our friends will be true blue forever. That the roof over our head will shield us from the elements.

And then inflation hits. Our car breaks down. The marriage goes sour. Our body ages and begins to betray us in ways we never could have imagined. We lose our job and can't find one that pays the same. A friend betrays us. A flood ravages our home.

The only one who will deliver us, save us, help us, strengthen us, shield us, be faithful to us, keep us afloat no matter what, is God. He alone is our strength, rescuer, help, courage, safety, and refuge.

Open the eyes of your inner warrior woman to the Lord. Trust in Him alone.

*YOU, LORD, ARE MY HELP AND REFUGE,
FOREVER AND A DAY.*

SILENCE! BE STILL!

*When Jesus woke up, he rebuked the wind and
said to the waves, "Silence! Be still!" Suddenly the
wind stopped, and there was a great calm.*

MARK 4:39 NLT

Jesus instructed His disciples to "cross to the other side of the
lake" (Mark 4:35 NLT). So they did, leaving the crowds behind them.
Before they knew it, they were caught in the middle of a storm.
Waves were crashing down over the boat. As the water rose, so
did the disciples' fear.

Meanwhile, Jesus was sleeping peacefully at the back of the
boat. His followers woke Him up, asking, "Teacher, don't you care
that we're going to drown?" (Mark 4:38 NLT).

Jesus rose from the cushion His head had been resting on, and
He silenced and stilled the wind. Immediately there was a great
calm. Afterward He asked the disciples if they had no faith—even
after all they'd seen Him do and heard Him say.

Perhaps you too are wondering where God is. Maybe you think
He's sleeping on the job. Take a moment to remember who Jesus
is, who His Father is. Let Him speak to all that's on your mind.
Allow Him to calm the chaos in your heart—to remind you to be
still and know that He is God.

*STILL THE WORRIES IN MY MIND, LORD. CALM
MY TURBULENT HEART. REMIND ME THAT
BECAUSE YOU ARE WITH ME, ALL IS WELL.*

TRUST, HOPE, WAIT

Our inner selves wait [earnestly] for the Lord; He is our Help and our Shield. For in Him does our heart rejoice, because we have trusted (relied on and been confident) in His holy name. Let Your mercy and loving-kindness, O Lord, be upon us, in proportion to our waiting and hoping for You.

PSALM 33:20–22 AMPC

What has your inner warrior woman been doing lately? Is she waiting sincerely for God? Is she putting all her hope in Him? Does she see God as her divine help and impenetrable shield?

God has so many blessings in store for you, so many promises to fulfill. When you trust in Him—with all your heart, soul, mind, and strength—He *will* come through. He will open doors you'd considered nailed shut. He will supply whatever you need whenever you need it—if you live with the confidence that His blessings are on their way, that His love is streaming down upon you, that His mercy will meet you around every corner.

The more you hope and wait on God, the more He will fulfill all your desires, supplying all you need and more. Begin today.

THANK YOU, LORD, FOR BEING MY HELP AND
SHIELD. FILL MY HEART WITH REJOICING
AS I HOPE IN AND WAIT ON YOU.

TAKE COURAGE

They were all terrified when they saw him. But Jesus spoke to
them at once. "Don't be afraid," he said. "Take courage! I am
here!" Then he climbed into the boat, and the wind stopped.

MARK 6:50–51 NLT

Need some courage? Take it! Jesus is with you! And He has an abundant supply.

When you are facing a challenge and have no inner confidence, you may feel as if the battle is already over. But Jesus is telling you it isn't. He wants you to remember that no matter how frightened your inner warrior woman may be, the fight isn't over when He is there—or rather, when you recognize or remember that He is there. With you.

When fear comes knocking at your door, don't run. Instead, invite Jesus into your boat, your life, your heart, your mind, your soul. Recognize that His power resides within you. Remember that He is there with you no matter where you go or what is happening. Regardless of outer circumstances, He resides within you and will help you, ease you, encourage you. For He is the source for all the strength and courage you could ask for or imagine. And with that strength and courage you can do all He calls you to do, to become the fearless warrior woman you already are.

HERE I AM, LORD, TO DRAW ON THE ABUNDANT
SUPPLY OF COURAGE YOU PROVIDE. BECAUSE YOU
ARE HERE WITH ME, I WILL NOT BE AFRAID.

THE SOUL'S SANCTUARY

You are my shelter, O Eternal One—my soul's sanctuary!
Shield me from shame; rescue me by Your righteousness.
Hear me, Lord! Turn Your ear in my direction. Come quick!
Save me! Be my rock, my shelter, my fortress of salvation!
You are my rock and my fortress—my soul's sanctuary!
PSALM 31:1–3 VOICE

Sometimes you need God to respond in a hurry, to quickly bend His ear down to your lips. When the danger you're facing is imminent, it's time to remember that no matter what the outer woman faces, your inner woman is safe in God.

Your inner self has one place it can run, one refuge in which it is protected and secure. That's in God. He alone is your rock, shelter, and fortress, your soul's sanctuary, a place where nothing evil or dark can touch you.

In times of chaos and calm, express your confidence in God, that He does indeed hear your prayer. Praise Him for being your rock, shelter, and fortress. Continually remind yourself that God alone is your soul's place of refuge, a place where it can and will be safe, unharmed, protected, calm, cool, and collected.

YOU, LORD, ARE THE REFUGE MY SOUL SEEKS. COME QUICKLY! GIVE ME SHELTER! FOR YOU ONLY ARE MY ROCK, MY FORTRESS, MY SOUL'S SANCTUARY.

GOD HOLDS TRUE

*The Lord says, "I will guide you along the best pathway for your
life. I will advise you and watch over you." . . . For the word
of the Lord holds true, and we can trust everything he does.*

PSALM 32:8, 33:4 NLT

The Bible contains hundreds of stories showing us how God keeps
His promises, all the ways in which His Word holds true. Then there
are the psalms that provide words we can use when our spirit desires
to speak to His. The Bible also contains proverbs that give us the
wisdom we need to walk God's way, to follow His lead.

When you have lost your way, when you need guidance regarding the best path to take, go to the Word. For those stories and
songs that have been written and told and retold are there to teach
us, encourage us, and give us hope (Romans 15:4).

When you understand that God's Word holds true, your trust
cannot help but grow. When you see how God has taken care of
people in the past, your anxiety will fade away and your courage
grow.

When you're seeking the right pathway, seek God. Trust that
in Him you will find all you need and all you didn't even know you
needed.

*LEAD ME IN YOUR WORD AND WAY, LORD,
AS I TRUST IN YOUR GUIDANCE, ADVICE,
AND PROTECTION. IN JESUS' NAME, AMEN.*

BE STILL, BE CALM, AND SEE

"Be still, be calm, see, and understand I am the True God.
I am honored among all the nations. I am honored over
all the earth." You know the Eternal, the Commander
of heavenly armies, surrounds us and protects us; the
True God of Jacob is our shelter, close to His heart.

PSALM 46:10–11 VOICE

Today and every day, God invites you to pause. To pull yourself out of the world and into His kingdom. For the only true place of peace and sanctuary is in God. He alone can calm your inner woman.

Too often we don't make enough time for God—not just Bible reading and prayers and praises, but allowing ourselves to sit in silence in the presence of the true God, the one who created us, loves us, protects us, provides for us, listens to us, dreams for us, plans for us, and oh so much more.

God wants to pull you close, to nestle you against His heart, to shelter you from all storms. Allow Him to do so today and every day. Take this moment to allow your inner warrior woman to connect with the Eternal One. To be still before Him. Be calm. And see.

HERE I AM, LORD, STILL BEFORE YOU. HELP ME
MELT MY SPIRIT INTO YOURS. HOLD ME
CLOSE TO YOUR HEART AS WE SPEND THESE
QUIET MOMENTS TOGETHER AS ONE.

AN OPEN INVITATION

Then Jesus said, "Let's go off by ourselves to a quiet
place and rest awhile." He said this because there were
so many people coming and going that Jesus and his
apostles didn't even have time to eat. So they left by
boat for a quiet place, where they could be alone.
MARK 6:31–32 NLT

Life can get hectic. Sometimes you may not know whether you're coming or going. Your schedule is overrun with to-dos. The house needs to be cleaned, clothes washed, car serviced. The kids have soccer games, youth group, band practice, and club meetings. The boss wants you to finish a project yesterday. You have worship team practice, a Sunday school lesson to prepare, or a board meeting to attend.

There doesn't seem to be enough hours in your day to rest. Yet that's what Jesus calls you to do. Jesus extends to you an open invitation to go off with Him, away to a quiet place, and rest awhile. There, in Jesus' presence, in the quiet of alone time with Him, your inner warrior woman will regain the calm, courage, and confidence she needs to walk the road God has put before her.

O LORD, THE BUSYNESS OF LIFE HAS TAKEN ITS TOLL.
LEAD ME TO THAT QUIET PLACE WHERE I CAN FIND
SOME PEACE AND REST IN YOUR PRESENCE, WHERE I
CAN BE REFRESHED, RENEWED, AND REVIVED IN YOU.

HOPE FOR YOUR FUTURE

*I know the thoughts and plans that I have for you, says
the Lord, thoughts and plans for welfare and peace and
not for evil, to give you hope in your final outcome.*
JEREMIAH 29:11 AMPC

As a boy, Joseph had dreams about his brothers and father bowing
to him (Genesis 37). But when he related those dreams to his sib-
lings, they got angry, threw him in a pit, and sold him to traders.
From there he was bought as a slave for the house of Potiphar, an
officer of the king of Egypt.

Yet even enslaved at Potiphar's house, a long way away from
his home, Joseph prospered. Why? Because God was with him and
"made all that he did to flourish and succeed in his hand" (Genesis
39:3 AMPC). Thus, Potiphar put him in charge of his entire household
and everything else he owned.

But then some other "bad luck" came Joseph's way when
Potiphar's wife unjustly accused him of rape (Genesis 39:17–19).
The angry husband threw Joseph in prison. Yet even there, "the
Eternal One remained with Joseph and showed him His loyal love
and granted him favored status with the chief jailor" (Genesis
39:21 VOICE).

Never doubt that God has a plan for your life. He will be with
you through what seems like bad times and make them work out
for good!

THANK YOU, LORD, FOR BEING WITH ME THROUGH ALL
MY DAYS, FOR GIVING ME HOPE FOR THE FUTURE!

STICK CLOSE TO GOD

The chief jailor, like Potiphar, didn't need to worry
about anything that was in Joseph's care because the
Eternal One was with him. And whatever Joseph did
worked out well because the Eternal made it so.

GENESIS 39:23 VOICE

Joseph was in prison, not knowing how long he'd be kept there. Yet he continued to trust in God. And because he trusted, God was with him and made things work out well for him, no matter where he landed.

While Joseph was imprisoned, Pharaoh sent his baker and cupbearer to the dungeon. There they "happened" to meet Joseph. The servants each had a dream one night. The next morning, Joseph offered to explain the meaning of the dreams to them, saying, "Don't interpretations belong to God?" (Genesis 40:8 HCSB). He told the cupbearer that the king would reinstate him. Joseph asked the cupbearer to remember him, to tell Pharaoh about him, to help him get out of the dungeon. Yet Joseph spent two more years in prison before he was released.

No matter how bad a situation may be in your life, keep your courage by sticking close to God. Keep the faith, knowing that God is moving behind the curtain to work out the best for you—and all His children.

LORD, THANK YOU FOR BEING WITH ME, FOR
WORKING THINGS OUT FOR GOOD. GIVE ME THE
COURAGE AND PATIENCE TO CONTINUE WALKING
WITH YOU NO MATTER WHAT TOMORROW BRINGS.

LIVE IN HOPE!

"I am Joseph your brother whom you sold into Egypt.
But don't feel badly, don't blame yourselves for selling me.
God was behind it. God sent me here ahead of you to
save lives. . . . God sent me on ahead to pave the way. . .
to save your lives in an amazing act of deliverance."
Genesis 45:5, 7 msg

The king of Egypt had had two dreams that his wise men couldn't explain to him. That's when Pharaoh's once-imprisoned cupbearer *finally* remembered Joseph as a great interpreter of dreams. And Joseph was called into Pharaoh's presence.

Joseph explained that Pharaoh's dreams were God's way of telling him there would be seven years of plenty followed by seven years of famine. Joseph then suggested Pharaoh store up the plenty to prepare for the years of famine that would follow.

Joseph's wisdom so impressed Pharaoh that he made him his second in command, putting him in a position to save not only the people of Egypt but his own family who came to live there! It was God who was behind all that happened to Joseph, turning his brothers' evil into something good.

Warrior woman, live in hope, knowing that "those who trust in the Lord will lack no good thing" (Psalm 34:10 nlt).

MY HOPE, MY CONFIDENCE, MY HEART,
MY TRUST IS IN YOU, LORD! ONLY YOU!

SURE AND FEARLESS

God is our shelter and our strength. When troubles seem near, God is nearer, and He's ready to help. So why run and hide? No fear, no pacing, no biting fingernails. When the earth spins out of control, we are sure and fearless.

PSALM 46:1–2 VOICE

God's strength and protection are closer than you think. That is the message of Psalm 46, the message we all need to hear, remember, and take to heart.

Psalm 46:2–3 (VOICE) reminds us that even "when mountains crumble and the waters run wild. . .even in heavy winds and huge waves, or as mountains shake," we can be sure and fearless. Why? Because "the True God never sleeps" and, in fact, "has already been at work" (verse 5 VOICE). Because "the Eternal, the Commander of heavenly armies, surrounds us and protects us" (verse 7 VOICE) with His love, His power, His strength, and His presence.

Even though the world may look as if it is falling apart, God's isn't. He is still in control. He has you under His wings. So there is no need to be afraid. Instead, trusting in God, walking with Him, following His lead, you can be "sure and fearless."

KNOWING THAT WHEN TROUBLE IS NEAR YOU ARE NEARER, LORD, GIVES ME HOPE, STRENGTH, COURAGE, AND CONFIDENCE. THANK YOU FOR YOUR PRESENCE AND THE PEACE IT BRINGS ME.

GOD-GIVEN SPIRIT

God did not give us a spirit of timidity (of cowardice,
of craven and cringing and fawning fear), but [He has
given us a spirit] of power and of love and of calm and
well-balanced mind and discipline and self-control.

2 TIMOTHY 1:7 AMPC

Finding yourself cowering in the corner? Feeling too afraid to take that step of faith? Here's what the Lord wants you to know: God has given your inner warrior woman not a "cowardly spirit but a powerful, loving, and disciplined spirit" (2 Timothy 1:7 VOICE).

No matter what challenge you're facing, no matter what duty lies before you, remember that you are God's daughter. You need not consider shrinking from whatever He has laid on your heart and mind to do. Don't worry about pleasing people. Don't allow the dread of danger regarding man's opinion of you to keep you from doing what you have been called to do.

Call on the power of the Holy Spirit to help you do what seems undoable. Tap into the strength of the Spirit to lift others up, to love the unlovable, to think clearly, to keep yourself on the right road.

You, warrior woman, are a creature of God more than man. His Spirit lives within you. You can do whatever He calls you to do. Just step forward in faith, courage, and strength, trusting God with every step you take.

I'M WALKING WITH YOU, LORD, IN YOUR
SPIRIT, KNOWING THAT IN YOU AND
WITH YOU I CAN DO ANYTHING.

HEAVENLY REALITIES

[Elisha] answered, Fear not; for those
with us are more than those with them.
2 KINGS 6:16 AMPC

God had given His prophet Elisha the ability to know and relay to the king of Israel what military tactics the king of Aram was whispering in his bedroom. In this way, Elisha's warnings were benefiting Israel time and time again.

Furious, the king of Aram sent a military force to Dothan to capture Elisha. One morning the prophet's young servant woke up and went outside, startled to see horses and chariots all around the city. Panicked, he ran to Elisha.

Elisha told his servant not to worry. After all, there were many more on their side than on the side of the opposition. Then he prayed, asking God to let his servant "see heavenly realities" (2 Kings 6:17 VOICE). As the servant's eyes were opened, he saw "the mountain was covered with horses and chariots of fire surrounding Elisha" (2 Kings 6:17 VOICE). Elisha then prayed for the Lord to blind the soldiers, and He did, and Elisha then led the army of Aram away.

When you're faced with an enemy that seems overwhelming, pray, asking God to open your eyes so that you can see His heavenly realities and gain the wisdom to lead the enemy away.

LORD, OPEN MY EYES TO YOUR PRESENCE,
POWER, AND PROTECTION SO I CAN
SEE THE REALITIES OF HEAVEN!

THE GOD WHO CARRIES

*When you were still in the womb, I was taking care
of you. And when you are old, I will still be there,
carrying you. When your limbs grow tired, your eyes
are weak, and your hair a silvery gray, I will carry
you as I always have. I will carry you and save you.*
ISAIAH 46:3–4 VOICE

False gods are dead weight. Those icons are heavy material objects that must be hauled all over the place, from pedestal to pedestal, by mules, camels, trucks, and trains. The true God, the Eternal One, the one who created you, isn't a god that needs to be carried. He's the God who does all the heavy lifting.

God cared for you while you were in your mother's womb. He took care of you when you were in the cradle. He held your hand while you took your first steps. He was there when you said your first word, and He will be there when you say your last.

Even when you are old and gray, when your body begins to fail you, God never will. He will always be by your side, giving you comfort, leading you by the hand, and carrying you. Saving you. Delivering you. Just as He always has.

May this truth comfort, pacify, and strengthen the warrior woman within you.

*THANK YOU SO MUCH, LORD, FOR ALWAYS BEING
WITH ME, CARRYING ME THROUGHOUT MY LIFE.*

WALK STRONG

"Be strong. Take courage. Don't be intimidated.
Don't give them a second thought because GOD,
your God, is striding ahead of you. He's right there
with you. He won't let you down; he won't leave you."
DEUTERONOMY 31:6 MSG

Moses knew he wouldn't be leading the Israelites into the promised land (Deuteronomy 31:2). That task now fell upon Joshua's shoulders. But before he and they parted company, Moses encouraged the people, telling them some things that would help them not just to get through the days ahead but to take on a way of being because of who God is and what He would be doing.

As one of God's people, this advice holds true for you. Today and every day, be strong. Exercise courage. And do not allow anyone or anything to intimidate you, for there is no reason for you to be intimidated. You have the Creator of the universe, the most powerful force visible or invisible striding ahead of you, clearing the path in which you are to walk. He lives within you by His Spirit, so, He, the almighty God, will neither let you down nor leave you. Claim these truths and take on a new way of being. Walk strong, warrior woman!

THANK YOU, LORD, FOR THIS MESSAGE. WITH YOU
ENCOMPASSING ME, CLEARING THE PATH, STRIDING
BESIDE ME, I CAN DO ANYTHING. IN YOU I FIND
MY STRENGTH AND CLAIM MY COURAGE.

NO GRUDGES, PLEASE

I urge Euodia and Syntyche to iron out their differences and make up. God doesn't want his children holding grudges.

PHILIPPIANS 4:2 MSG

Nothing can sap your strength and distort your wisdom more than holding a grudge.

Esau held a grudge against Jacob for stealing their father's blessing (Genesis 27:41). After their father Jacob died, Joseph's brothers feared that Joseph was holding a grudge against them and would soon repay them for the suffering they'd caused him (Genesis 50:15). Yet to Joseph's credit, he forgave his brothers, considering that what had happened to him had been part of God's plan all along.

Herodias, King Herod's wife, held a grudge against John the Baptist (Mark 6:19). It ate away at her to the point where, at the first opportunity, she plotted to have John beheaded.

We're not to hold grudges (Leviticus 19:18). When we do so, we open the door to evil (2 Corinthians 2:9–11). Besides, God "doesn't endlessly nag and scold, nor hold grudges forever. He doesn't treat us as our sins deserve, nor pay us back in full for our wrongs" (Psalm 103:9–10 MSG). So, if you have resentment and hatred toward someone who has wronged you, let them go. Give them to God. Allow forgiveness and love to take over. Doing so will not only nurture and strengthen your inner warrior woman but will please God as well.

LORD, YOU'VE LOVED ME DESPITE OF MY WRONGS.
GIVE ME THE POWER TO LOVE OTHERS DESPITE THEIRS.

ALWAYS WITH US

"I am God, the God of your father," the voice said.
"Do not be afraid to go down to Egypt, for there I will make
your family into a great nation. I will go with you down
to Egypt, and I will bring you back again. You will die in
Egypt, but Joseph will be with you to close your eyes."
GENESIS 46:3–4 NLT

Joseph had revealed himself to his brothers. Then he invited them and their father, Jacob, to leave their land of famine and come and live in Egypt where they would be well cared for.

Thrilled, the brothers went back home to tell their father that his son Joseph was not only alive but was a leader in Egypt. And he wanted them to come live with him. In response, Jacob said, "My son Joseph is alive! I must go and see him before I die" (Genesis 45:28 NLT).

Jacob and his children prepared to leave. The night before their departure from Beersheba, God spoke to him, telling him not to be afraid. He promised Jacob that He would be with him wherever he went—*and* bring him back again.

God makes the same promise to you. You need never fear for He is always with you. Whether you are preparing for a new job, a long journey, a new endeavor, a new relationship, or death, there's no need to fear. God will be with you and bring you back, no matter where you are or where you go.

THANK YOU, FATHER, FOR BEING WITH ME EVERYWHERE.

A SIMPLE PRAYER

They were trying to intimidate us into quitting.
They thought, "They'll give up; they'll never
finish it." I prayed, "Give me strength."
NEHEMIAH 6:9 MSG

Nehemiah had finished rebuilding the wall around Jerusalem. The only thing left was to install the gates. Yet his enemies continued their efforts to intimidate him. First, they tried to get him to meet with them. But Nehemiah suspected they were planning to hurt him, so he refused. Four times they pestered him. And four times he denied them.

Israel's enemies' fifth attempt was to send Nehemiah a letter accusing him and the Jews of planning to rebel. That's really why the wall had been rebuilt. They insisted Nehemiah sit down and talk with them. Nehemiah replied, "There's nothing to what you're saying. You've made it all up" (Nehemiah 6:8 MSG). Then he simply prayed, "Give me strength."

Your best source of strength is God. And all it takes to receive that strength is a simple prayer such as, "Give me strength."

God doesn't need a fancy speech from you. He doesn't need you to throw yourself on the floor or to moan and cry. All He needs are the words "Give me strength." And you shall receive it.

LORD, GIVE ME STRENGTH.

ARISE RADIANT

O LORD. . .come to my aid. . . . O LORD, you know all
about this. . . . "Great is the LORD, who delights
in blessing his servant with peace!"
PSALM 35:1, 2, 22, 27 NLT

God already knows what problems you face. He knows what challenges lie before you. Yet still He wants you to speak to Him. He wants you to put your problems into words. To come to Him and get all that's worrying you, frightening you, causing you anxiety, off your chest. To leave all your cares at His feet. When you do, when you let God know all that's troubling you, laying it out before Him, you will find the peace that He promises.

Consider all the prayers the Bible contains, the way God's people lay their problems before Him and then hear His answer, witness His response. With each prayer they grow more faithful, more trusting, more peaceful, more courageous.

Sometime after pouring her heart out to God, Hannah's face glowed, became radiant. That's what God wants to see on you. A face relieved of worry and trouble. A face that is a light unto itself, drawing others to God.

Tell God what's on your mind. Tell Him what He already knows, and rise refreshed, having left all things in His hands.

LORD, HEAR MY WORDS AS I POUR OUT MY HEART.

BE OPENED!

*Jesus. . .put his fingers into the man's ears. Then, spitting
on his own fingers, he touched the man's tongue. Looking
up to heaven, he sighed and said, "Ephphatha," which
means, "Be opened!" Instantly the man could hear perfectly,
and his tongue was freed so he could speak plainly!*

MARK 7:33–35 NLT

People brought a deaf man who also had a speech impediment to
Jesus, begging Jesus to heal him. So Jesus led the man away from
the crowd. There He put His fingers into the man's ears. Then He
spit on His fingers and touched the man's tongue. He then looked up
to heaven, perhaps saying a silent prayer to His Father. Sighing, He
said, "Be opened!" In an instant, the man could hear—and speak!

Jesus comes to you in the same way. He takes you aside, away
from the crowd, asking that you open your heart to Him, that you
open the door on which He is knocking. He wants in so He can
sit with you, talk to you, listen to you (Revelation 3:20). But no
conversation can happen if you keep your door shut to His knock.
He asks, "Are your ears awake? Listen. Listen to the Wind Words,
the Spirit blowing" (Revelation 3:22 MSG).

"Be opened!"

HERE I AM, LORD, OPENING MY DOOR TO YOUR
KNOCK. OPEN MY HEART AND MY EARS. HELP ME
HEAR WHAT THE SPIRIT IS SAYING. GIVE ME THE
STRENGTH AND COURAGE THAT I NEED TO RESPOND!

ENCOURAGERS

*"Be strong and courageous! Don't be afraid or discouraged
because of the king of Assyria or his mighty army,
for there is a power far greater on our side! He may have
a great army, but they are merely men. We have the LORD
our God to help us and to fight our battles for us!"*

2 CHRONICLES 32:7–8 NLT

King Sennacherib of Assyria had invaded Judah. When King Hezekiah realized he was intent on attacking Jerusalem as well, he talked things over with his military counselors and advisers. They decided to stop the flow of springs outside Jerusalem, cutting off a brook that ran through some fields so Sennacherib wouldn't have plenty of water.

Hezekiah then had broken sections of the city wall repaired, towers erected, terraces reinforced, and lots of weapons and shields made. He placed military officers over the people and had them come before him at the city square. Then Hezekiah encouraged them with the words in today's verses, telling them to be strong and take courage because God was on their side to help them and fight their battles.

We need encouragers. And there's no greater or better encourager than God's Word. When you need strength and courage, when you need peace and calm, when you need to know you're not alone, read the Word, the stories, the Psalms and Proverbs. Feed your warrior woman well so that she ceases to become a woman worrier.

*LEAD ME TO THE VERSES MY INNER WARRIOR WOMAN
NEEDS, LORD. NOURISH ME! STRENGTHEN ME! LOVE ME!*

GOD'S UNFAILING LOVE

I will be glad and rejoice in your unfailing love, for you have seen my troubles, and you care about the anguish of my soul. You have. . .set me in a safe place. . . . The LORD protects those who are loyal to him. . . . So be strong and courageous, all you who put your hope in the LORD!

PSALM 31:7–8, 23–24 NLT

In today's verses, David reveals what brings him joy: the fact that God loves him beyond measure. He's seen David's troubles and cares about the anguish he's experiencing.

Ever been there? So full of trouble, so overwhelmed with anguish? It's in those moments that we are perhaps the most frightened. When we feel the most alone.

The remedy is entrusting our life to God, putting our spirit into His hands, knowing it is safest there (Psalm 31:5). It's only by rejecting the false idols in our lives and trusting in the Lord completely that we find relief from all that's attempting to drag us down or keep us in the darkness (verses 6–7). It's only then that we can once more hope in God, and, in doing so, find the courage and strength we need in His light.

> I ENTRUST MY LIFE, SOUL, SPIRIT,
> HEART, AND MIND TO YOU, LORD.

YOUR SONG

The Eternal is with me, so I will not be afraid of anything. . . .
I was pushed back, attacked so that I was about to fall,
but the Eternal was there to help me keep my balance.
He is my strength, and He is the reason I sing;
He has been there to save me in every situation.

PSALM 118:6, 13–14 VOICE

No matter what situation you face, know that God is with you. And because He is with you, there is no need to be afraid. . .of anything.

The world can throw a lot of things our way, things we never expected to happen. Yet even in those trying times, we can turn to the one who made us, saved us, and waves us on to the victory line. Just when you think you're about to fall, call on God. He'll be there to help you keep your balance.

Today and every day, make God your partner in life. Seek Him in the morning, at noon, and in the nighttime—and any other hour in your day when you need His help, His strength, His courage. Make Him your song, the one you sing in every situation. Then victory over challenges, leaps over obstacles, solutions to problems will be yours for the making and taking.

> *YOU, LORD, ARE ALL I NEED, FOR YOU ARE*
> *MY STRENGTH, MY COURAGE, MY SONG.*

CALL ON GOD

Rise during the night and cry out. Pour out your
hearts like water to the Lord. Lift up your
hands to him in prayer, pleading.
LAMENTATIONS 2:19 NLT

When you need help, when you are in the middle of a battle that seems unwinnable, when your human efforts have failed miserably, call on God. Rise up. Cry out to Him. And pour out your heart, telling Him everything that's weighing you down, frightening you, sapping your strength. Lift up your hands and spirit to God, pleading for the help, strength, and courage you need.

God would have you never give up, never surrender, when you're walking in His will and way. Consider all the psalms in which the psalmists pour out their heartaches. How often they see trouble, no way out of a situation, and lift their voices up to the Lord, knowing only He can give them the strength they need to see things through.

What is it that you're wrestling with? Where in your life do you need God's strength, His power to persevere? When was the last time you prayed to Him for help? In what areas of your life do you need the courage to do the right thing?

In this moment, rise up. Pour your heart to God. Lift up your hands and soul to Him. Tell Him what you need, this moment, this hour, this day of your life. You will not walk away empty-handed.

LORD, I CRY OUT TO YOU! HEAR MY PRAYER!

PEACE BE WITH YOU

That Sunday evening the disciples were meeting behind locked doors because they were afraid of the Jewish leaders. Suddenly, Jesus was standing there among them! "Peace be with you," he said. As he spoke, he showed them the wounds in his hands and his side. . . . Again he said, "Peace be with you."

JOHN 20:19–21 NLT

No tomb can hold Jesus. That's what Mary Magdalene learned earlier that day.

Now, in the evening of the same day, the disciples learned that locked doors are no challenge to Jesus either. He can do anything. No matter where you are or what you're going through, Jesus can reach you, help you, remind you that you are not to be troubled. You are not to be afraid.

Each time Jesus comes to you, He brings you His peace. He is the source of all calm, all that you could ever need. When you're frightened, panicked, trying to rationalize what is going on in your life, Jesus comes to you to offer His peace.

Whenever fear comes knocking at your soul, imagine Jesus coming to you. Reach out and touch Him, allowing His peace to be poured out upon you, to be a balm to your soul and spirit. You will be blessed if you believe (John 20:29).

LORD, I COME TO YOU SEEKING PEACE. POUR IT OUT UPON ME. MAY IT CONSTANTLY BE WITH ME.

THE GOD PERSPECTIVE

*"You are seeing things merely from a
human point of view, not from God's."*
MARK 8:33 NLT

God told Moses to send twelve spies into the promised land to check things out. So he did, picking one man from each tribe. They were to come back with a report about what the land was like, who lived there, and how many lived there. He told them to be courageous and to bring back fruit from the land.

After forty days, the men returned, reporting that the land was bountiful, flowing with milk and honey. But they also reported that the people living there were powerful, and some were giants. This alarmed the Israelites. Nevertheless, two spies, Caleb and Joshua, were of the opinion that they could conquer the land—and that they should go right away and do just that.

The other ten spies vehemently disagreed, saying, "There we saw the Nephilim [or giants], the sons of Anak, who come from the giants; and we were in our own sight as grasshoppers, and so we were in their sight" (Numbers 13:33 AMPC). In other words, because these men saw themselves as small, the giants did as well.

When you see things from a human perspective, your vision is distorted, fear emerges, and weakness takes over. The promise lies in seeing things from God's point of view.

LORD, HELP ME SEE THINGS WITH YOUR EYES,
KNOWING THAT WITH YOU, ANYTHING IS POSSIBLE.

TAKING THE PROMISED LAND

Do not rebel like this against the Eternal. Don't be afraid
of the land's inhabitants. It is we who will devour them!
They are now defenseless, and nothing can protect them from
the Eternal, who is with us. You don't need to be afraid of them!

NUMBERS 14:9 VOICE

The people of God were in an uproar, crying at the top of their lungs, tearing their clothes, weeping into the night. They began accusing Moses and Aaron, saying, "If only we had just died in Egypt or somewhere along the way in this wilderness. . . Wouldn't it be good just to go back to Egypt?" (Numbers 14:2–3 VOICE).

Joshua and Caleb tried to tell them there was no need to be afraid. After all, God was on their side. The inhabitants of the land would be defenseless against His strength and power. But their words fell on deaf ears.

Perhaps you see giants in your own life. You cower before them. You figure that you may as well retreat rather than face them. But you need to remember that God is with you. With Him on your side, you can take the promised land. If you allow Him to take on the battle, He will fill you with all the courage and strength you need to do what seems impossible.

HELP ME, LORD, TO ALWAYS REMEMBER
THAT WITH YOU BY MY SIDE, I CAN
REACH THE LAND OF YOUR PROMISES.

A WALL OF FIRE

The Eternal One says, "Instead of a wall of stone,
I will be a wall of fire protecting her all around,
and I will be the shining glory within her."
ZECHARIAH 2:5 VOICE

You need no man-made walls around you, no material protection, because God is with you. He is your defense, the one who will shield you from harm.

At the same time God shields you, He makes His glory very apparent by doing mighty deeds not only within you but around you. God has made clear that "no instrument forged against you will be allowed to hurt you, and no voice raised to condemn you will successfully prosecute you. It's that simple" (Isaiah 54:17 VOICE). The warrior woman who resides within you needs to hear these words. She needs to take them in as truth. For this is her reality when she is walking with God.

Such a wall—"horses and chariots of fire"—was Elisha's guard when a huge army came against Israel, because his eyes and heart were open to "heavenly realities" (2 Kings 6:17 VOICE).

And the psalmist tells us, "Just as the mountains around Jerusalem embrace her, the Eternal, too, wraps around those who belong to Him—for this moment and for every moment to come" (Psalm 125:2 VOICE).

Today, take these words to heart, continually whispering them to the warrior woman within.

BE MY WALL OF FIRE AROUND ME, LORD.
BE THE SHINING GLORY WITHIN ME.

ALL YOU COULD ASK

*Jacob (to Joseph): I didn't know if I would ever see
your face again, but now God has given me more than
I hoped: He has let me see your children too.*

GENESIS 48:11 VOICE

Word was brought to Joseph that his father was gravely ill. So he went to see Jacob, bringing with him his two sons, Manasseh and Ephraim.

Seeing the offspring of his favorite son, Jacob expressed how God had given him more than he could ever imagine. Not only was he able to see Joseph again but his sons as well. On his deathbed, Jacob described his God as "the God before whom my ancestors Abraham and Isaac walked, the God who has been my shepherd all of my life and still to this day, the messenger who has rescued me from all harm" (Genesis 48:15–16 VOICE).

That God, the God of those who have gone before, is your God as well. He's the one who walks with you now and always, the one who is your shepherd, leading you, caring for you, guiding you, protecting you, providing for you. That God is the one who continually rescues you from harm and "the God who can do so many awe-inspiring things, immeasurable things, things greater than we ever could ask or imagine through the power at work in us" (Ephesians 3:20 VOICE).

Believe that and you will uncover all the courage and strength your warrior woman needs.

*IN YOU, LORD, I HAVE ALL THAT I COULD
ASK OR EVER IMAGINE—AND MORE!*

BULLY TALK

"What's the price of two or three pet canaries? Some loose
change, right? But God never overlooks a single one. And he
pays even greater attention to you, down to the last detail—
even numbering the hairs on your head! So don't be intimidated
by all this bully talk. You're worth more than a million canaries."
LUKE 12:6–7 MSG

"Bully talk" can come from any quarter. When Moses tried to break up a quarrel between two Hebrews, one of the men said, "Who do you think you are, telling us what to do?" (Exodus 2:14 MSG). When he led the Israelites through the wilderness, they constantly grumbled and complained to him. Even his brother, Aaron, and sister, Miriam, spoke against him, saying, "Is it only through Moses that GOD speaks? Doesn't he also speak through us?" (Numbers 12:2 MSG).

Bullying can also come from within when we don't realize our value. When God called Moses to lead the Hebrews out of Egypt, Moses didn't think he was leadership material; he didn't think anyone would believe him, trust him, listen to him. He thought he didn't speak well enough to lead God's people and finally asked God to send someone else (Exodus 3:11–4:13).

You are valuable to God. You are worthy to answer His call. So tell those who would intimidate you to take a hike.

THANK YOU, LORD, FOR GIVING ME THE COURAGE
TO IGNORE THE BULLY TALK—WHETHER IT COMES
FROM OTHERS OR IT'S OF MY OWN MAKING.

STRENGTH FOR EVERYTHING

*I have strength for all things in Christ Who empowers
me [I am ready for anything and equal to anything
through Him Who infuses inner strength into me;
I am self-sufficient in Christ's sufficiency].*

PHILIPPIANS 4:13 AMPC

Regardless of the situation you're in or how you are feeling—
physically, mentally, or emotionally—you can have all the strength
you need. Jesus Christ is the one who empowers you, infusing
strength into your mind, body, spirit, and soul. And because of
that minute-by-minute infusion, you can be content no matter what
is coming against you.

Imagine living content regardless of the circumstances you
face, the challenge before you, the obstacle that stands in your way.
It sounds like a dream come true! And yet it is no dream. Jesus
is real. What He can give you is real. All you need to do is throw
off all the self-sufficiency within you. To accept your weaknesses,
become conscious of your missteps. To accept God's grace. Then
you will find the strength that is perfect in weakness.

In this moment, ask God for strength. Then take what is given,
over and over again.

*THANK YOU, JESUS, FOR THE STRENGTH THAT
EMPOWERS ME TO DO WHAT YOU WOULD
HAVE ME DO. I AM READY FOR ANYTHING
AS I LIVE AND BREATHE IN YOU.*

PUTTING THINGS RIGHT

Commit your path to the Eternal; let Him direct you.
Put your confidence in Him, and He will follow through
with you. . . . Be still. Be patient. Expect the Eternal to
arrive and set things right. . . . So turn from anger. Don't rage,
and don't worry—these ways frame the doorway to evil.
PSALM 37:5, 7–8 VOICE

All the cares that you keep to yourself, the worries that consume you, can be handed over to God. Share them with God. Let Him know each and every little detail that has you in a fretful fever. Worrying only saps you of energy—physical, spiritual, and mental.

Fretting can sometimes even crowd God out. For when you're thinking of nothing but all the bad things that are happening or could happen, you're not focusing on Him. You cannot see Him walking toward you, nor can you hear Him saying, "Woman, that load is too heavy for you. Put it all on Me."

Let all the troubles that are weighing you down slide off your back and onto God's. Let Him tell you what to do and where to go next. Rest assured that He will see you through this day and all the others to come. Then be still, waiting patiently for Him to put everything right. After all, that's His job.

I'M HANDING OVER TO YOU ALL MY TROUBLES, LORD, KNOWING THAT YOU WILL MAKE ALL THINGS RIGHT IN YOUR TIME.

NO-FALL ZONE

The LORD directs the steps of the godly. He delights
in every detail of their lives. Though they stumble,
they will never fall, for the LORD holds them by the hand.

PSALM 37:23–24 NLT

What a beautiful picture these verses paint. You can envision yourself as a little girl walking with God, allowing Him to lead you to where He would have you go. As you travel along the way, He admires your smile, your step, your laugh, your dress. He is delighted in the way you hold your head, the things you are curious about, the way you hold your hand firmly in His, following every little tug, changing your direction at every prompting from Him.

Suddenly you trip. You're not sure what you've tripped over, but you feel as though you are starting to fall. The ground is rising up before you, getting closer and closer. You begin to imagine what it might feel like to slam into that concrete. But before you know it, you feel the strong arm of the Lord lifting you up, keeping you from falling on your face.

Warrior woman, know that as you walk with God, as you let Him direct your steps, you never need to fear a thing—because He's got you and will never let you go. Nothing can snatch you out of His strong, firm hand (John 10:28).

I'M KEEPING MY HAND FIRMLY IN YOURS,
LORD. LET'S WALK TOGETHER. FOREVER.

THAT EXTRA MILE

"Do not resist an evil person! If someone slaps you on the right cheek, offer the other cheek also. If you are sued in court and your shirt is taken from you, give your coat, too. If a soldier demands that you carry his gear for a mile, carry it two miles. Give to those who ask, and don't turn away from those who want to borrow."

MATTHEW 5:39–42 NLT

Jesus is for love and peace, not conflict and war. Yes, there is evil in this world. Yet we're not to resist it. Instead, if someone behaves badly enough to slap us on the cheek, we're supposed to offer up the one yet unharmed. If someone takes our shirt, we're to give him our coat as well. And if someone forces us to walk a mile, we're to go one more with her.

We're to be a giving people. A loving people. A peace-making people. A helping people. This may seem like a frightening path to walk. Yet it is the journey Jesus wants us to make if we are walking His way.

To bolster your confidence in this regard, simply ask Jesus to infuse you with not just His strength but His courage. And then determine to do one good deed a day—to glow with both the light and love Jesus has poured into you.

WITH YOU BY MY SIDE, JESUS, I KNOW I'LL HAVE THE CONFIDENCE TO WALK THAT EXTRA MILE—OR TWO.

BOOST OF FAITH

And Jesus said, [You say to Me], If You can do anything?
[Why,] all things can be (are possible) to him who
believes! At once the father of the boy gave [an eager,
piercing, inarticulate] cry with tears, and he said, Lord,
I believe! [Constantly] help my weakness of faith!

MARK 9:23–24 AMPC

The disciples couldn't drive an evil spirit out of a boy. So his father appealed to Jesus for help.

Jesus asked the man how long the boy had been having this issue. The father said, "From childhood. . . . But if You can do anything, have compassion on us and help us" (Mark 9:21–22 HCSB).

Jesus couldn't believe His ears. He responded, " 'If You can'? Everything is possible to the one who believes" (Mark 9:23 HCSB).

The father cried out that he did indeed believe Jesus could heal his son. Then he asked that Jesus *constantly* help his weakness of faith, his many doubts.

You may have found yourself in these same circumstances or even now feel as if your faith needs a boost. If so, ask Jesus for help. Constantly, if necessary. Ask Him to give you the strength and grace to put all your confidence in Him, knowing He will do so if you would only rely on Him for everything.

LORD, I NEED A BOOST OF FAITH. HELP ME HAVE THE
STRENGTH TO PUT ALL MY CONFIDENCE IN YOU.

GOD, YOUR STRENGTH

O Lord, do not stay far away! You are
my strength; come quickly to my aid!
PSALM 22:19 NLT

When you need strength, where do you go? To the gym? To a self-improvement course? To a friend's house? You need not go anywhere other than to God and His Word. For it is God who is the source of your strength. He is the one to call on when you need a boost.

When God parted the sea for the Israelites, Moses called Him his strength, song, and salvation (Exodus 15:1–4). The psalmists agree that God is our refuge and strength in times of trouble (Psalm 46:1–3). That it's God's promises and encouragement found in His Word that give us the strength to stand (Psalm 119:28).

Proverbs 18:10 reminds us that God is a strong fortress the godly can run to for safety. Isaiah tells us God gives strength to the weary, that those who trust in Him will renew their strength. He reminds us that we need not fear because God will not only strengthen and help us but hold on to our hand (Isaiah 40:29–31, 41:9–10).

In your weakness, Jesus Christ's power works best (2 Corinthians 12:9–10). Be strong in the Lord and His power (Ephesians 6:10–11), knowing you will be able to do all things through Christ who strengthens you (Philippians 4:13).

IN YOU AND YOUR WORD, LORD,
I TAKE UP ALL THE STRENGTH I NEED!

TAKING UP COURAGE

Joseph, he of Arimathea, noble and honorable in rank
and a respected member of the council (Sanhedrin),
who was himself waiting for the kingdom of God,
daring the consequences, took courage and ventured
to go to Pilate and asked for the body of Jesus.

MARK 15:43 AMPC

Joseph of Arimathea was a disciple of Jesus. But he'd kept it a secret because the Jews had intimidated him. Yet after Jesus died on the cross, Joseph found the courage needed to ask Pilate for His body (John 19:38).

All of Jesus' disciples had taken off. So here stood Joseph, in this moment, *his* moment, the moment he'd been destined for. He took up the courage he'd found in God and boldly asked Pilate for the body of Jesus, his teacher, healer, and friend. Jesus, who had also been cursed, mocked, and condemned to die.

It was a risk. But Joseph knew he was made for this moment. He took up the courage God offered and was blessed with the granting of his petition.

There are times when you may have to risk the consequences. Yet those are the moments you have been made for. And God will not only grant you all the courage you need but bless you with the desired result.

LORD, WHEN MY MOMENT COMES, I PRAY YOU WILL GIVE ME THE COURAGE TO DO WHAT YOU HAVE DESTINED ME TO DO. AND BLESS ME WITH A FAVORABLE RESULT.

STAYING STEADFAST

So here is what I want you to do: conduct yourselves as true and worthy citizens of the Anointed's gospel. . . . Don't be paralyzed in any way by what your opponents are doing. Your steadfast faith in the face of opposition is a sign that they are doomed and that you have been graced with God's salvation.

PHILIPPIANS 1:27–28 VOICE

Jesus would have us emulate Him. That means loving one another, continually forgiving as God forgives us, being honest in our dealings, speaking words of peace, looking for the best in all, and having compassion for each other, to name a few.

So when others try to hurt you, insult you, shame you, or simply shout in your face, take that higher road. Don't run and hide nor repay insult with insult and evil with evil. Instead, repay evil with good.

In all things, God would have you keep your peace. And look to Jesus. *He* is the one you are to adore. *He* is the one you want to imitate. *He* is the light shining through you, the light of love that will change the world one heart at a time. Stay steadfast in your faith, and you will be given all the courage and strength and love you need to be like Jesus.

> LORD, WHEN OPPONENTS APPROACH,
> HELP ME KEEP TO YOUR WAYS.

COMING TO OUR SENSES

"That brought him to his senses. He said, 'All those farmhands working for my father sit down to three meals a day, and here I am starving to death. I'm going back to my father. I'll say to him, Father, I've sinned against God, I've sinned before you; I don't deserve to be called your son. Take me on as a hired hand.' "

LUKE 15:17–19 MSG

Jesus told the story of a man who had two sons. The younger of the two asked for his share of the estate that would come to him at his father's death. The father agreed. The son then went off to a place far away and squandered all his father's money.

Just as his money ran out, the land suffered a famine. The son began to starve. He begged for a job and was hired to feed pigs. Famished, the pig slop began to look good to him. That was when he came to his senses.

Sometimes it takes a desperate situation to force us into realizing how far we have drifted away from home, from our Father. But then, when we do come to our senses, we must not fear going to God and admitting our mistake and asking His forgiveness. Instead, we must take up our courage and humbly admit our sin and submit to the Father, who loves us more than we can ask or imagine.

LORD, I COME TO YOU, HEART IN HAND,
AND BEG YOUR FORGIVENESS.

GREETED BY LOVE

So he got up and came to his [own] father. But while
he was still a long way off, his father saw him and was
moved with pity and tenderness [for him]; and he ran
and embraced him and kissed him [fervently].

LUKE 15:20 AMPC

You, woman of God, have a Father like no other. When you finally come to your senses and go to Him, ready to humbly admit your mistakes and missteps, prepared to ask for His forgiveness and what little love He may have to spare for you, He sees you—even while you are still a long way off. He is moved with compassion for you. Tenderness and pity rise within His heart. And He runs to greet you, to hold you, to kiss you, to encompass you with His love.

Then you begin the speech you have repeatedly rehearsed in your mind, the speech in which you tell Him that you have drifted away from Him and sinned. That you don't even deserve to be called His daughter. But He's not even listening to your prepared and well-rehearsed words. He's too busy celebrating your return!

Never allow your inner warrior woman to be afraid to come to God, to confess her mistakes, to ask for His forgiveness. Simply remember that your God is love personified. And He will rejoice to welcome you back into the fold!

THANK YOU, LORD, FOR YOUR LOVE THAT RUSHES
TO GREET ME. I AM OVERWHELMED.

NEVER FEAR

*And I give them eternal life, and they shall never lose it
or perish throughout the ages. [To all eternity they shall
never by any means be destroyed.] And no one is able to
snatch them out of My hand. My Father, Who has given
them to Me, is greater and mightier than all [else]; and no
one is able to snatch [them] out of the Father's hand.*

JOHN 10:28–29 AMPC

Warrior woman, take heart! Nothing can separate you from God
and His love. In God, you have eternal life. And no one and no thing
can ever take away or destroy that life.

Nor can anyone—man or devil—snatch you out of Jesus'
hand! God has given you to Jesus, to live and love in His care. He's
the good shepherd whose voice you know and follow. And God
is greater, mightier, more powerful than anything or anyone else!

May these truths remind you of the protection you are under.
May you always keep in mind that God is your certain refuge and
strength in this life—and the next!

No robber can steal you from this destiny. No thief can come
in and surprise Jesus or overcome God by force. This is how much
God loves you. This is how tightly Jesus holds you. This is how
mighty the Spirit is within you.

Never fear. God is always near.

*BECAUSE YOU ARE SO NEAR AND HAVE SUCH A
FIRM GRIP ON ME, LORD, I WILL NEVER FEAR.*

FIVE GUIDELINES FOR THE WARRIOR WOMAN

Be on guard. Stand firm in the faith. Be courageous.
Be strong. And do everything with love.
1 CORINTHIANS 16:13–14 NLT

The apostle Paul exhorts his readers to do five things as the people of God. The first is to be on the lookout concerning not just dangers but temptations that might come our way. We must be aware of what's going on within and without. The second is to keep the faith. To remember we are sheep and Jesus is our good shepherd, and to continue to trust in Him to keep us on the right path, protect us, and lead us. The third is to be brave. Not to cower at any evil or trouble that comes our way but to face it, knowing that God surrounds us with His wall of love. The fourth is to be strong, allowing God's Word to fortify our faith and our relationship with Him. Lastly, we are to live a life of love, allowing it to inform and affect both our words and actions. For God is love.

Every day remind your inner warrior woman of these guidelines. To be alert, stand firm in the faith, be brave and strong, and do all with love, remembering that God is there to help you all the way.

HELP ME, LORD, TO BE ALERT, FAITHFUL, BRAVE, AND STRONG. BUT MOST OF ALL, TO LIVE A LIFE IN AND OF LOVE. IN JESUS' NAME I PRAY, AMEN.

THE SOURCE OF
ALL COMFORT

As a mother soothes her child, so I will comfort you.
ISAIAH 66:13 VOICE

That's it. That's all you need to know, really. That as a mother soothes her child, God will soothe you. He will give you all the comfort you need. Always. Whenever.

There is no bond like that between a mother and her child. After all, she carries the child for nine months. Within her body. Even during pregnancy, when the baby has not fully formed, you may see a pregnant woman lovingly caressing her tummy. She may sway back and forth, as if rocking the unborn child to sleep.

Then, when the world greets the child, she is very protective, shielding the baby from harm, keeping her safe, for the infant is helpless in this world. When the baby cries, tiny nerves in the mother's breasts are automatically stimulated, prompting her breast milk to flow. Eager to feed the child, she answers its cry and pulls the child to her breast, bringing it the comfort of food and love.

When you are afraid, when you are distressed, when you feel weak, when you are hungry for love, go to the one who is always there, whose compassion is stimulated at the sound of your cry. And be comforted.

*LORD, HEAR MY CALL. BLESS ME WITH
YOUR TENDER COMFORT AND LOVE.*

THE RIGHT PATH

This is what the Lord says: "Stop at the crossroads and look around. Ask for the old, godly way, and walk in it. Travel its path, and you will find rest for your souls."
JEREMIAH 6:16 NLT

You are a traveler, a sojourner, a pilgrim on this earth. And there may be times when you come to a crossroads, unsure of which path to take. Some path may look good to you, yet when you embark upon it, you may find it leads you into danger. So before taking that self-chosen path, stop. Look around. And find the path that will lead you to God, a place where you can find rest for your soul, the rest that Jesus promises when He invites you to come to Him (Matthew 11:28–30).

Just as God led the Israelites safely through the sea, just as Jesus shepherded His followers to a place of rest, just as others followed the Holy Spirit and were rescued, the Three-in-One will lead you to safety, to a green pasture, to still water that runs deep (Isaiah 63:11).

Don't tremble at the crossroads. Instead, appeal to God, asking Him for the ancient path of rest, of peace. The path that leads you to Jesus, who tells you, "I am the path, the truth, and the energy of life" (John 14:6 VOICE).

LEAD ON, JESUS. LEAD ON!

THE EVERYWHERE GOD

It is the Lord Who goes before you; He will [march] with you;
He will not fail you or let you go or forsake you; [let there be
no cowardice or flinching, but] fear not, neither become broken
[in spirit—depressed, dismayed, and unnerved with alarm].

DEUTERONOMY 31:8 AMPC

Moses spoke the above words in his goodbye speech to the Israelites. For they would be going into the promised land without him.

These same words apply to you and your life, your way, your journey upon this mortal coil. Just as Moses wanted to give his people this assurance, God desires to give it to you.

Know that God is everywhere. His presence is wherever you are, nearer than you might imagine. Yet while He is marching with you, God is going before you. He's checking out the scene, spying out the land, looking for any hidden traps or dangers, shadows lurking around the corner or on the other side of the mountain.

While God walks with you and goes before you, His Spirit is residing within you (Romans 8:9). So no more cowardice or flinching. Rest in the truth that God's presence is before, in, and beside you, keeping your warrior woman within from becoming alarmed or unnerved. As you walk on, God reminds you, "Be strong. Take courage. I'll be right there with you."

THANK YOU, GOD, FOR BEING EVERYWHERE—
BEFORE, BESIDE, AND WITHIN ME!